SO-BRE-927

37330

Mallarmé

Mallarmé: SELECTED PROSE POEMS, ESSAYS, & LETTERS

TRANSLATED & WITH AN INTRODUCTION BY Bradford Cook

BALTIMORE: The Johns Hopkins Press: 1956

© 1956, The Johns Hopkins Press, Baltimore 18, Md.

Distributed in Great Britain by Geoffrey Cumberlege
Oxford University Press, London

Printed in the United States of America by Vail-Ballou Press

Library of Congress Catalog Card No. 56–8065

Simmons College Library

to

E K C

and

M H C

" . . . *comme on ne fait qu'un avec l'instrument de ses sortilèges.*"

JUN 3 '73
'73

Contents

Translator's Preface

Roger Fry, George Moore, Stefan Georg, Rainer Maria Rilke, Alfonso Reyes, Wallace Fowlie, Arthur Ellis, Stuart Merrill, Elizabeth Sewell, Grange Woolley [1]—these and lesser known writers and scholars have sought the signal and elusive victory of translating Mallarmé into their several languages. Some have rendered the letter with understandable intent to introduce the poet to their countries as plainly as possible. And yet just as no language more unwillingly than the French yields up its "reticences and refusals," as Gide calls them, so perhaps no writer in that tradition seems so jealous as Mallarmé of the strange and exquisite life he gave his mother tongue.

Mallarmean prose language is complex, abstract, condensed, quiet, outwardly cold (choppy and ugly upon occasion), but capable of extraordinary beauty, grace, and eloquence. In most of these essentials it resembles the language of Racine or Pascal. My principle in this book has been to raise Mallarmé's voice, to clarify and concretize whenever I feared that the virtual power, passion, and beauty of his thought might elude the English-speaking reader whose eye and ear feel more at home with the linguistic sumptuousness of Shakespeare or Gerard Manley Hopkins than with the dry, tortured, or seemingly wordless aphorisms of La Rochefoucauld.

For those virtualities are, I believe, the marrow and spirit which

1 Roger Fry in *Stéphane Mallarmé. Poems* (New York, New Directions, 1951); George Moore in *Confessions of a Young Man* (London, Swan Sonnenshein, 1899); Stefan Georg in *Blätter für die Kunst*, 1892 and 1905; Rainer Maria Rilke in *Gesammelte Werke* (Leipzig, Insel-Verlag, 1927), Vol. VI; Alfonso Reyes in *Mallarmé entre nosotros* (Mexico, Tezontle, 1955); Wallace Fowlie in *Mallarmé* (Chicago, University of Chicago Press, 1953) and *Mallarmé as Hamlet* (Yonkers, The Outcast Chapbooks, No. 16, 1949); Arthur Ellis in *Stéphane Mallarmé in English Verse* (London, Jonathan Cape, 1927); Stuart Merrill in *Pastels in Prose* (New York, Harper and Bros., 1890); Elizabeth Sewell in *The Structure of Poetry* (London, Routledge and Kegan-Paul, 1951); Grange Woolley in *Stéphane Mallarmé* (Madison, New Jersey, Drew University, 1942).

must somehow seize us before we can claim full knowledge of this very great mind. The involutions and obscurity of his language were the intricacies and temper of a delicate instrument increasingly refined by the artist as the most suitable means to his visionary end. But that instrument belongs inalienably to the French language. In English, another and necessarily imperfect means must be found; for we too have our refusals.

In observance of my principle, I have razed some of the magnificent syntactical structures of Mallarmé's prose, disintegrated long periods with a view to clarity, supplied verbs which he preferred merely to imagine, strengthened adjectives weak-seeming but strongly intended, ignored his delightful, sometimes meaningful, but usually grotesque punctuation—and still hoped to find in English some miniature structure reminiscent of those destroyed, some abstractness correspondent with his, some tone of pride to match his pride, some insight into his original and distant worlds; still hoped that, in the midst of sacrilege, some essence of the man remained or, like his Hamlet, some "jewel intact in the midst of chaos."

In explanation of the choice of texts, I would first express my hope that the prose-poems will be read as illustrations of Mallarmean esthetic theory as well as for themselves alone. *Autumn Complaint* —like the omitted *Phenomenon of the Future, The Pipe, Poor Pale Child,* or *Winter Shuddering*—comes from the years when, though still undelivered from the Baudelairian influence, Mallarmé was nonetheless absorbing it into his own originality. *The Demon of Analogy* looks into the creative process and remains a highly original work. *Glory* combines the humorous and meditative in one of Mallarmé's last and most appealing attempts in this genre. *The White Water-Lily* is, in my opinion, the most beautiful prose-poem in the French language. Despite the excellence and amused preciosity of certain of its passages, the extreme complexity and diffuseness of *Declaration at the Fair* led me to omit it. Together with *Reminiscence* and *An Interrupted Performance,* it treats the circus or histrio theme explicit in *The Punished Clown,* implicit in *Hamlet.*

With the exception of *Conflict, Displays,* and *Limited Action*— uneven works, although at their best (especially in the last-named) they are first-rate Mallarmé—I have translated all the important essays on literature and poetics. The only main sections entirely omitted (save for occasional reference in the notes) are the so-called *Offices* and *Grands Faits Divers.* However interesting these pieces may be to scholars (exposition of Mallarmé's theories on religion, rite, etc.), they consist generally of a kind of ugly, jagged shorthand highly resistant to clarification.

Of Mallarmé's twelve essays on the theater or ballet, I have chosen the three which critics generally accept as the most finely written and best known. In any case, there is a good deal of repetitiousness within this section of his work. The substance and even some of the expressions of *Ballets,* for example, recur in *Another Dance Study* and *Mimic.* Mallarmé's comments on *Macbeth* are unfortunately without much interest.

The list of works on individual artists looks promising: Villiers de l'Isle-Adam, Verlaine, Rimbaud, Théodore de Banville, Maupassant, Tennyson, Poe, Whistler, Manet, Berthe Morisot, Wagner. But in some (e.g., *Maupassant, Tennyson*) the man becomes a pretext for the discussion of ideas better expressed elsewhere. In others (e.g., the very disappointing *Rimbaud*), Mallarmé is content with anecdotes about a writer whom he appears never to have understood very deeply or with whom he had little in common. Still others (e.g., *Manet, Whistler*) seemed too short and insubstantial. On the other hand, it was with considerable misgivings that I finally decided to omit the long, diffuse, uneven, but still magnificent *Villiers de l'Isle-Adam,* and the *Banville,* which contains one or two of Mallarmé's finest stylistic achievements. The very brief, but alternately moving and explosive *Edgar Poe* has been partially rendered in the notes for *Music and Literature.*

For the choice of Mallarmé's letters, I refer the reader to the notes for *Ideas on Poetry.*

The unfinished and highly technical *Diptych, Notes,* and *Igitur,* finally, were felt to be of little interest to the general reader.

RIVERSIDE, CALIFORNIA   *Bradford Cook*
MARCH, 1956

Acknowledgments

Acknowledgment is gratefully made to the heirs and literary executors of Mallarmé and to the Librairie Gallimard for permission to translate selections from *Œuvres Complètes de Stéphane Mallarmé* (Bibliothèque de la Pléiade, 1945); to Dr. Henri Mondor of the French Academy for permission to translate selections from *Propos sur la Poésie* (Edition du Rocher, 1953) and to quote from *Vie de*

Mallarmé (Gallimard, 1941); to A. Messein *éditeur* for permission to translate *Lettre Autobiographique;* and to the University of Chicago Press for permission to quote Wallace Fowlie, *Mallarmé.*

I wish to thank Professor Wallace Fowlie of Bennington College, Mr. Jackson Mathews of the Bollingen Foundation, Professor W. Y. Tindall of Columbia University, and Professor Philip Wheelwright of the University of California at Riverside for reading the translations. The encouragement of these well-known authorities on Symbolism has been most welcome.

Several of my colleagues on the Riverside campus of the University of California have given generously of their time and counsel. I am particularly indebted to Professors William Elton, Donald Greene, Herbert Lindenberger, and L. Marshall Van Deusen.

It is my hope, above all, that these pages will convey my deep and lasting gratitude to Professor Henri Peyre, Chairman of the French Department of Yale University, who first revealed Mallarmé to me and urged me to undertake this work.

The longest and most patient hours were given by my wife. For such as these, thanks are never quite fittingly expressed.

Introduction

Martyr to an absolute and mystic to a beauty which were perhaps no more than the extraordinarily abstractive power of his own thought (this was his tragedy), Stéphane Mallarmé endures in the chaste and harrowing image of the poet met at midnight with his demon and tempted toward the re-creation of his universe: met— like the most reverent and aware of victims of the Word—with prescience of defeat which, nonetheless, he sometimes overcame and so composed a perfect poem.

What lived and moved incarnate in his vision, he never truly said or ultimately defined through his esthetic. The esthetic itself appears as the attempt and inevitable failure not merely to define for others but to discover for himself as well what he thought he saw. We come away from his work with a sense of the majestic and the beautiful, mysteriously divorced from any explicable cause or effect. The work is haunted everywhere by the invisible angels of his Absolute, his Ideal, his Truth Herself Incarnate. And while the possibilities of the French language have been marvelously expanded through the slender volume of his poetry, rarely have the limitations of language been so piteously demonstrated as in the spectacle of this artist driven back time and again to the repetition and capitalization of these impalpable leitmotifs.

For his vision is never linked to living man, nor yet to any apprehensible god. The common life of mind and conscience pales before his dream of beauty. His "Infinity"—was it merely the chance focus of a centripetal esthetic?—seems not quite our own; our world of nature not quite the "Nature" to which he bitterly and merely concedes "existence." He invites us to the contemplation of a universe incommensurate even with the most fanatical of our faculties. The imagination gladly flies with him but never comes to rest.

Mallarmé saw nothingness. The restraint and distilled horror of his early letters establish the reality of that vision. But over against the saints, who travel their abyss with hopeful eyes turned ahead to heaven, stands this figure of incredible loneliness—terrified, yet

xiii

so inseparable from his source of terror that he takes it for the All and devotes the last thirty years of his life to its reconstruction through poetry. "After I found Nothingness," he writes in 1866, "I found Beauty." Which surely means that, in order to avoid suicide or madness, he was compelled to find beauty *in* that nothingness. Such is the heart of his metaphysic. Just how it preceded the esthetic, and whether it was to a degree suggested and intermittently revived by art, we cannot know.

By his own confession, Mallarmé wrote poems and prose-poems only as approximations of his nothingness; essays only as explanations. And because nothing mattered to him save his dream, we must ideally look through and beyond whatever page we read, as he himself, in writing it, tries to mirror or conjure the great X.

But fortunately for the poet's sanity, plain literary enjoyment also exists and is to be had in the finite world of excellent black on white. The absolute, envisionable in the spirit, expressible in the flesh, is finally more satisfying in its imperfect state. Language became his host, guided the mind's eye toward the "threatening peak of the Absolute" (so movingly evoked in *Richard Wagner*), then mercifully lowered it to earth and to the written word.

The Mallarmean esthetic seeks to resemble the simplicity and complexity of the divine. Nothingness begins and ends it; in the midst lies poetry. Like the "virgin space divided of itself in solitude," which constitutes mystery in literature, the beginning is chaos and pure chance; these are "vanquished word by word" until nothingness and silence become "genuine and just"—until the poet's vision is becalmed. Genesis must be his goal on earth, while the inner ear is listening for the silences of horror and peace at either end of the eternity. But what was begun—what *was*—before the Word began? And what will be?

"A kiss would kill me," cries Hérodiade, the heroine of one of his earlier and more famous poems, "were it not that beauty itself is death." Indeed, despite the intervening poetry, the second silence seems hardly distinguishable from the first; each partakes of the general "virginity"; and all his nothingness smacks of a unique death abstracted from all obvious agony, melancholy, or antecedent life. This is the single-minded and ultimately inaccessible Mallarmé, whom friends and critics have, with their awe, almost canonized. And that is why the most cursory reader is soon absorbed in the underlying oneness of his elaborate work. For what is the cold virginity or sterility of Hérodiade; the whiteness of the water-lily; the absence of the lady at the river bank; the faun's disappear-

ing nymphs; the "pure pathless delight" of Mlle Mallarmé's fan;
those "spiritual instruments" which are the blank spaces of the
Book; Hamlet, "prince of promise unfulfillable"; the impuissant,
timeless swan immersed in the very elements of frost and scorn
which are his incarnation; the silence of Saint Cecilia at her harp;
the "Nothingness Which is the Truth" of *Ideas on Poetry;* the ever-
present mirror; the constellation; the fire; the precious stones; the
spiritual nakedness of the poet in *Verlaine;* or Mallarmé himself
cut off from earth in the eighteen-sixties and "quite dead now" on
"the purest glaciers of Esthetics": what is any page of this work but
the beautiful, monotonous, imperfect sign of that sacred "something else" in *Music and Literature* or of the "disquieting gleam"
in *Mystery in Literature*—themselves imperfect expressions of the
infinite *Rien*—which the poet, philosopher, or mystic calls God,
Idea, Ideal, Nothingness, Emptiness, Abyss, Horror, and so on
through the history of the greatest minds at bay? So, in his power-
lessness, a Mallarmé is reduced to imperfect reproduction through
poetry, imperfect definition through prose; reduced to the "act of
folly," as he called the poetry of his *Coup de Dés*—just as a thinker
of ancient times was reduced to the "philosophy of Plato." None
have been more aware than they that beauty on earth is a second-
best.

Nothingness, then, because it is Mallarmé's metaphysical constant, becomes his esthetic unity. The "real" or "unreal" (whatever
meaning these words may now contain) is a One which the artist
can approach or imitate only through the many, like the Response
which a Baudelaire would elicit through the correspondences of
several faculties. The Mallarmean esthetic in action is the countless
series of exchanges and correspondences between this One and
many. How to produce the many (how to "make something out of
nothing"; here Mallarmé the stylist and metaphysician are scrupulous heirs to the French classical tradition)—how to produce the
many and how to return to the One: these are the interpenetrative
and chief problems.

Accordingly, his prose works are offered not alone as a conjura-
tion, but as intricate and abstract definitions of that esthetic. A funeral oration, a critique of free verse, a review of the dance or drama
—the most varying subjects and approaches are interpreted as radii
of the one invariable circle.[1] We feel the presence of that circle; but
we are unable to analyze it, since no single part has meaning or

[1] The main divisions observed in this volume are therefore arbitrary, as all
such divisions of Mallarmé's work must be.

existence save in its relation to the rest. In short, talk as he will of overcoming the ineffable, Mallarmé is forced by the very nature of his esthetic into the indefinable.

One of the most frequent and engaging representations of this dynamic esthetic, this "symphonic exaltation," is the pyrotechnic: where the virtual, gamesome, compressive fire of mystery or unity bursts forth into art and celebration at some "forbidden, thunderbolt height of heaven" in *Music and Literature* or *Crisis in Poetry*. So, too, the "volatile scattering which we call the Spirit," the ubiquitous gleams from precious stones, or even the dying scintillations of his prose: all much stronger when they lay still unemitted in his thought. Mallarmé always returns to the age-old *aspiration* of the spirit. From the humorous love-birds of *Ballets* to the "dialectic of Verse" in *Solemnity,* the sense of the vertical pervades his work: principles "spring up" from "Poetry—the only source"; rhyme, tending to unify the multiplicity of verse, "flutters and rises from earth"; the arrows of verse shoot high to heaven; the ballerina's "dizzying satin slippers" fly up to the Idea.

More intricate than fireworks are the formations idealized in *Hamlet* and *Ballets: "The symbolic relationship of characters, either to themselves or to a single figure";* or the ballerina star with her satellites, all performing a "mobile, unending, ubiquitous synthesis." Every genre (itself a multiple of one great art, as we shall see) is defined by its own particular arabesque. One of Mallarmé's most original rites (outlined to a few of his friends and rather evasively presented in the closing pages of *Solemnity,* and again in the late essays *Sacred Pleasure* and *Sequel*) called for a Hamlet-"hero"— simultaneously actor and priest—appearing alone on an evanescent stage, reading from "the book of himself." This solitude could then be surrounded and multiplied by a chorus chanting an ode of indeterminate size and structure. Mallarmé's evasiveness in this matter is particularly regrettable; a detailed and concrete reinterpretation of the Greek drama would surely have provided the finest illustration of his total esthetic. Failing his version, we can only imagine a vast spectacle combining elements of the Catholic rite, the Hamlet-hero, and the Greek drama (the latter two were never absent from his thought). These were all the ingredients of his ideal: lyric poetry, dirge and triumph; the ode with its infinite variations; the altar at the center of the orchestra, surrounded by the singing and dancing chorus and coryphaeus (thus satisfying the author of *Solemnity, Ballets,* and *Crisis in Poetry*); secret communications between altar, coryphaeus, priest of Dionysus, and actor-priest on the *skene;* flutes and organ (the latter for "the crisis moments of the soul," the former for variations and "knowing dissonances"); the Great Book as host; and finally the highly trained audience (for the author of *The Evolution of Literature, Richard Wagner,* and *Hamlet).*

The Book: A Spiritual Instrument and *Crisis in Poetry* explain a like process for the written work. Absolute unity will be the letter of the alphabet: sacred first element of a literary algebra envisioned in *Ballets* and the *Coup de Dés.* The letter multiplies to form the more practical unity of the word; the word progresses and "mushrooms" through the sentence, line, verse, paragraph, page, and book; then through all books up to the invisible level of the Great Work which Mallarmé imagines as being more or less consciously composed in collaboration by all geniuses. Thus, turned to words, the Word again becomes the Word in the cycle of ideal which is mobilized by art. Yet not so much a cycle as an arabesque: the multiplications are never purely linear, circular, or vertical; each to its proper position of beauty and harmony. A certain asymmetry of parts—"a scattering of ornaments"—makes for the final symmetry.

Indeed, in his consideration of the written work, Mallarmé will feel at liberty to make unity of any one of these dimensions. The alexandrine verse (accepted by his predecessors as the constant of their poetic language) will appear as the flexible, floating fixture of his art, blown to the limit of its radius along the newest directions of the poet's inspiration. Such, in part, is the "evolution of literature" and the "crisis in poetry." Increasing dissonances will demonstrate the ultimate need for consonance; "free" or "polymorphic" verse will threaten, but at last withdraw. French verse will be a single soul or "thyrsus" made of "strands" and "knots" and "meshes" to be knowingly woven or tangled. Or, again, paginal unity may assume the monster-form described in *Richard Wagner* and *Music and Literature,* bled and shaken into all the metamorphoses of poetic agony or exaltation—yet with no permanent loss of its original life—in order to "extend or simplify the world at will."

To all these ends, "typography becomes a rite." Nothing in the mechanics of the page can be left to chance, since the Book is a "spiritual *instrument.*" Certainly no esthetic has descended more deeply than Mallarmé's to the last details of the work of art; each unity in turn, from the letter to the Ideal, is religiously enthroned and served—perhaps to excess; yet the esthetic chain counts for its strength and beauty on the perfection of its most seeming negligible parts.

But the majestic unity is the Book itself. Even the Greek drama, ideal interplay of the many, must yield to the Great Work: to the silent, immovable, now hopeful One; to the occasional "tomb in miniature for our souls." This, for him, is the crossroads of metaphysic and esthetic, the unseen and suspected pyrotechnic; dark as death with pages closed; all brilliance and mobility when we look within. Gathered here, thought Mallarmé, the best of human faculties may somehow still the "irascible wind" borne from the abyss—from the nothingness which he called Truth whenever he despaired of poets' power. He defined this Book a thousand times; and still it lies beyond our intellectual, if not imaginative, grasp. Here, in an inconceivable harmony, he would converge the essences of all the arts, merge all minor forms (each with its arabesque of lesser unities) within the grand, single architecture of the absolute.

First is the drama with its latent ritualistic power; its intuitive audience, chorus, and mystic, monologuing, silent hero. Then comes the dance, pregnant with the "writhings" of the Chimaera-poem; the ballerina (human pyrotechnic "enveloped with lightning"), whom Mallarmé revered above all other forms of the poet, whenever he imagined her inscribing the geometrical beauty of her steps on the nothingness of air or shooting the magic words and numbers of no book to the receiving heavens, which would then convert them to a constellation victory over pure space. Then music (omnipresent in these essays), feminine and imprecise, veils and softens the harsh intellectual relief of the written word, infuses mystery everywhere, but withdraws whenever the poet of *Music and Literature* joins battle with the ineffable. In this way, all separate methods for the "production of happiness" collaborate in the "totality of universal relationships" (explaining, incidentally, why Mallarmé welcomed any new artist or art form—even Zola and free verse—from which he might cut still another facet, the better to receive, refract, then mirror all possible intricacies of his absolute).

The reader of *Art for All* may well look aghast at the assertion that *he* is the last, and by no means least, of Mallarmean unities. It is a standing joke—and perfectly in keeping with this esthetic—that Mallarmé expected everyone to be an intuitive and grammatical genius of the first rank. Nothing less than a "mastering glance" suffices to "link the scattered notes together." It is true, of course, that the elaboration which art provides lives and moves in isolation like the virgin Hérodiade or the constellation. "The initiative is taken by the words themselves," as Mallarmé insists in *Crisis in Poetry* and frequently repeats. True, again, it is that the mere *creation* of the elaborate would seem sufficiently to constitute a return to the One. So it may, in the abstract. But to a realm which was differently (though perhaps no less) abstract, Mallarmé consigned the poem and reader together; or, more gently (as in *Mystery in Literature*), he summoned them to their own "nuptials" and thus to the reproduction of the Ideal. The reading mind, in his view, literally absorbs the multiple work within its own unity. And so, for this rather demanding poet, the kingdom of the absolute is in each one of us; the assumed perfection of mind is capable of perfect joy; the "new religion in France," he exclaims in the closing pages of *Music and Literature,* "will be the heavenly instinct within each one of us, expanded to the dimensions of infinite joy."

What, then, of the infamous Mallarmean "mob"—the "pursuing pack" of vulgar newspaper reporters, dull students and professionals, "incompetent in all matters pertaining to the absolute"? Theoretically, again, they will sit (like the ideal audience of *Richard Wagner*) and, with their now impeccable faculties engaged in an arabesque of intellectual glances, multiply the ideal which they are witnessing around the altar or the stage. But from the "hoots and spitballs" in his classroom to the preposterous attacks of a Max Nordau, the reality of the mob and its considerably less than perfect faculties baited him from his tower and struck home on the idealist, who struck back with the usual arms of endangered genius: scorn and humor. Such essays as *Glory, Solemnity, Art for All,* or *Music and Literature* (in the middle portion), are swords drawn and sheathed by the poet who alternately sees and idealizes his public.

Esthetically disappointed and resigned, as he tells us in *Crisis in Poetry,* Mallarmé accepted the conclusion that his nothingness and One would be communicable only through the many. Now he was committed (like nature) to the intricate syntax long since synonymous with his art; to the demon of infinite analogy or arabesque imagery, in which tenor and vehicle become multiple equivalents, keep us guessing as to the origin, direction, and extent of the image, and so create the impression of singleness preserved by—or "set up as"—complexity. He was committed more generally to every imaginable trick of language; [2] to the "languages of the school, home, and market place" prescribed in *Music and Literature;* to the colloquial and esoteric; to the production of the *taste* of nothingness either by omissions, blanks, or abstractions—occa-

[2] R. G. Cohn's analyses of Mallarmé's vowel and consonant symbolic, ideograms, etc. are at least quantitative evidence.

sional irritants which the imagination can turn to subtleties and messages of extraordinary beauty; committed to the smile of resignation and sense of humor in *Glory,* confronted as he was with his own human limitations and the impossible task of poetry; committed nonetheless to dandyism, self-defense, or the mental aristocracy of *Art for All* in order to reduce such limitations.

Or did he merely feel committed, and was the esthetic a miscalculation? Is the process of complexity a basically obscuring process and (despite its dream of unity) an ultimately disunifying process, no matter how harmoniously conceived and executed? Is the metaphysical abstract improperly reproduced by the esthetic abstract? Must language be a host more palpable and direct, if we are to touch the hidden god behind? Should the seer have fulfilled his wish for silence and ignored the possessed poet of *Crisis in Poetry* for whom "nothing will endure if it remains unspoken"?

Critical comment on the Mallarmean esthetic has hitherto tended to begin—but it should rather end—with this question of the abstract, the complex, or the precious. It is from these effects that first impressions and critiques naturally derive; effects so pure of their kind, indeed, that minds foreign to Mallarmé's have risen with unusual haste and violence to the attack. A class of mind (inclusive of the best and worst) undoubtedly exists which wearies almost instantly of the ornate, the allusive, and the difficult. The prevalence of this reaction will always confine the reputation of a man who has been (and can be) truly admired only by the few who first catch the "disquieting gleam" and then will have no peace until they reach the source. Mallarmé's admirers can only hope that future readers will go beyond their weariness and get a second wind to carry them to the heights which are the proper starting point of his esthetic.

For preciosity and its variants *are principally effects;* or, to put the matter darkly, they are esthetic symptoms of the metaphysical malady contracted by the man who saw nothingness. To deplore such effects is natural—but idle, so long as they prepare and lead us toward the cause. To expect a Mallarmé to lead us *to* the cause is to expect an act of God. To this—as to all things most worth knowing—there can never be a mind or art quite adequate. If the vision of nothingness is worth knowing, then a kind of faith is needed in the necessary communicative instrument of the visionary. If we desire the truth about that vision, we cannot escape the touch of darkness, torture, or folly upon the man who saw or upon his art. But, in fact, the most differing minds *have been* prepared and led by this art which, in its own way, brought "not peace but a sword." And though, like Mallarmé himself on the Wagnerian mountain, they may have stopped half-way, the "threatening peak of the Absolute" was dimly visible, nonetheless.

Doubtless there were times—Mallarmé joked about them—when the esthetic became enamored of itself, as any great esthetic must: obscurity could be excessive and intentional; stylistic complexities could smother rather than embrace the vision; the vision itself may not always have been quite so demanding as the transcriptive art implies. But, on the whole, its gravity and immediacy remain, even as its mystery remains; all the years remain which he surrendered to it; the disquieting gleams still issuing from his poems cannot be the radiance of mere esthetic.

In short, the style *is* the vision in ways we do not know. *Ideas on Poetry* points particularly to the close relationship of metaphysical experience to esthetic formulation. Ideally, the experience should remain in isolation; art should withdraw. And, surely, Mallarmé's search for silence through art can be taken as a heart-rending desire to atone for the spiritual crime which art necessarily commits in its attempt to dismember the ineffable. Thus all details of his method are designed to cling as closely as possible to the silence of his experience. The question of the individual vision and its communication is answerable only in the particular.

But if his esthetic taste or duty ever hesitated, Mallarmé could always look for confirmation to the Parnassian ideal. While *The Evolution of Literature* and *Music and Literature* disapprove the poetic ambition to express rather than to suggest, they welcome the tendency to abstract, the metrical command, and the impersonality of the poet. Again, a history of French esthetic instinct must place Mallarmé—and he will go proudly—with such seventeenth-century "abstractionists" as Racine, La Bruyère, or La Fontaine. The qualities of his language, though more pronounced than theirs, are basically the same.

As poet and visionary, he stands somewhat apart from the nineteenth-century group of Hugo, Balzac, Baudelaire, and Rimbaud. His experience reaches us in so distilled a form that he sometimes seems outside of life. We feel safer and surer with the mysteries of Hugo's sea, Balzac's seething society, the Baudelairian sense of sin and foreign longings, and even with Rimbaud's "illuminations." For they at least plumb their mystic depths with flesh and blood, with the personal cry or curse.

But, for all its outward obscurities, Mallarmé's work has become one of the most beautiful and arresting evocations of purity that literature has ever had. This mind born to silence, rarity, and impeccable structure—all perfectly absorptive of our passions—was eminently Mozartean. Yet in this classicist, we sense not merely the continuance but, at last, the validity of the Romantic complaint; more in him than in the open grief of certain of his predecessors, we see the curse upon the poet, suspect that suicide was sometimes more than possible, and that the cemetery of the mind (witness the young author of *Weary of bitter rest*) was indeed dug nightly by the lamp.

As for our own time, Mallarmé presents the issue in a humorous and scornful tone. Contrasting the Realists and psychological novelists with the Symbolists, he observes the difference between "a corset and a beautiful throat." Twentieth-century literature—Surrealism excepted—has preferred the corset. We have gained intricate knowledge, destruction, despair, or a pitiful sense of hope for the naive phenomenon of "man alone." With our thirst for clarity, we have tended to lose vision and the thirst for beauty. Mallarmé preferred the "worth unknown, although its height be taken." Very few artists have gone to greater lengths than he to take that height; very few have known so well as he how untakable it is, yet how worthy of the foredoomed attempt.

PROSE POEMS

Autumn Complaint

EVER SINCE MARIA LEFT ME and journeyed to another star—was it Orion, Altaïr, or thou, young Venus?—I have always cherished solitude. How countless the long days I have spent alone with my cat! By "alone" I mean without a physical being; my cat is a mystical companion, a spirit. So I can say that I have spent long days alone with my cat; alone, too, with one of the last writers of the Latin decadence. For ever since that white creature's death, I have strangely, specially loved all things which can be summed up in the word "fall." My favorite season of the year, for example, is summer in those last languishing days which come just before autumn; and in the daytime my walking hour is when the sun rests before fading away, with its yellow copper rays upon the grey walls, its red copper rays upon the window panes. So, too, the literature in which my mind seeks lust will have to be the dying poetry of Rome's last moments, so long as it does not taste of the Barbarians' rejuvenating approach, or stammer forth the childish Latin offered by the first Christian prose works.

Well, I was reading one of these cherished poems (their col-

1

ored plates charm me more than the bloom of youth), and I was fondling the fur of that pure animal, when a street-organ began to play, languidly, melancholically beneath my window. It was playing on the long avenue of poplar trees whose leaves, even in spring, have seemed dreary to me ever since Maria passed through them for the last time, with candles. Yes, certainly, this is the instrument of the sad. The piano sparkles, the violin sheds light upon the anguished heart. But the street-organ, in the twilight of memory, has always made me dream with despera- tion. And just as it was murmuring some common, joyous air and filling the city's heart with gaiety (a worn and ancient air), why did its endless song go straight to my soul and, like a romantic ballad, make me cry? Slowly I savored it and forbore to throw a coin from the window—fearful of discovering, if I moved at all, that the instrument did not sing alone.

The Demon of Analogy

HAVE WORDS UNKNOWN—evil remnants of a meaningless phrase —ever sung upon your lips?

I went out of my apartment with the definite sensation of a wing gliding, languid and light, on the strings of an instrument which was then replaced by a voice speaking these words in a de- scending tone: "*La Pénultième est morte,*" in such a way that *La Pénultième* came at the end of the verse, and *est morte,* de- tached from that fateful suspension, ran uselessly on into the re- sulting emptiness of meaning. I took a few steps along the street and then, in the sound *nul,* I felt the taut string of the musical instrument: it had been forgotten, and now, surely, glorious Memory had just visited it with His wing or with a palm-branch. Now I had the key to the mechanism of this mystery; I smiled,

and with all my strength of mind I prayed for a different specula-
tion. Then the phrase came back again in virtual form; for it had
freed itself of that first touch of the wing or palm-branch; henceforth it would be heard through the voice. Finally, it came to be
uttered of itself and lived through its own personality. I was no
longer content merely to perceive it; I went along reading it
mentally as a rhyme; and once, to test it, I spoke it aloud. Soon
I was saying it in such a way as to make a pause after *Pénultième,*
which was a painful joy: I would say *"Pénultième,"* and then the
instrument's string, stretched taut in forgetfulness over the sound
nul, would seem to break, and I would add in a sort of litany:
"est morte." But I didn't stop trying to get back to more pleasant
thoughts; and, to be calm, I kept telling myself that *Pénultième*
is, of course, the lexical term which means the next to last syllable
of a word; that it had appeared simply as a hang-over from that
linguistic work which day by day breaks in upon my noble poetic
faculties, making them weep. But I was tormented by the very
sonority of those excuses, by the falseness emanating from those
facile statements. Now I was at bay, and I resolved to let the
gloomy words of the phrase wander of their own accord about my
lips. I went along murmuring in piteous tones: "The Penult
is dead, dead, quite dead, that desperate Penult," thinking that
I could thus relieve my anxiety and bury it (such was my secret
hope) in the growing expanse of the singsong. But suddenly,
magically, and to my horror (a very understandable magic, because of its nervous origin), as I watched my hand, mirrored in a
shop-window, making a downward and caressing gesture, I realized with a start that the voice was my own—the voice which I
had first heard and which was undoubtedly the one and only.

But what revealed the undeniable presence of the supernatural, and what set off the anguish which has since possessed my
usually masterful mind, was this: instinctively, I had been walking along the antique dealers' street; I looked up and saw that
I was standing in front of the shop of a violin maker; for sale
were old instruments hung on the wall, yellow palm-branches on
the floor, and ancient birds' wings hidden in the shadows. I fled

in madness from that place. It was probably my fate to remain in mourning for that inexplicable *Pénultième*.

The White Water-Lily

I HAD BEEN ROWING for a long time with a sweeping, rhythmical, drowsy stroke, my eyes within me fastened upon my utter forgetfulness of motion, while the laughter of the hour flowed round about. Immobility dozed everywhere so quietly that, when I was suddenly brushed by a dull sound which my boat half ran into, I could tell that I had stopped only by the quiet glittering of initials on the lifted oars. Then I was recalled to my place in the world of reality.

What was happening? Where was I?

To see to the bottom of my adventure I had to go back in memory to my early departure, in that flaming July, through the rapid opening and sleeping vegetation of an ever narrow and absentminded stream, my search for water flowers, and my intention of reconnoitring an estate belonging to the friend of a friend of mine, to whom I would pay my respects as best I could. No ribbon of grass had held me near any special landscape; all were left behind, along with their reflections in the water, by the same impartial stroke of my oars; and I had just now run aground on a tuft of reeds, the mysterious end of my travels, in the middle of the river. There, the river broadens out into a watery thicket and quietly displays the elegance of a pool, rippling like the hesitation of a spring before it gushes forth.

Upon closer examination, I discovered that this tuft of green tapering off above the stream concealed the single arch of a bridge which was extended on land by a hedge on either side surrounding a series of lawns. Then it dawned on me: this was simply the

estate belonging to the unknown lady to whom I had come to pay
my respects.

It was an attractive place for this time of year, I thought, and I
could only sympathize with anyone who had chosen a retreat
so watery and impenetrable. Doubtless she had made of this
crystal surface an inner mirror to protect herself from the brilliant indiscretion of the afternoons. Now, I imagined, she must
be approaching it; the silvery mist chilling the willow trees has
just become her limpid glance, which is familiar with every leaf.

I conjured her up in her perfection and her purity.

Bending forward with an alertness prompted by my curiosity,
and immersed in the spacious silence of the worlds still uncreated
by my unknown lady, I smiled at the thought of the bondage
she might lead me into. This was well symbolized by the strap
which fastens the rower's shoe to the bottom of the boat; for we
are always at one with the instrument of our magic spells.

"Probably just somebody . . ." I was about to say.

Then, suddenly, the tiniest sound made me wonder whether
the dweller on this bank was hovering about me—perhaps by the
river!—while I lingered there.

The walking stopped. Why?

Oh, subtle secret of feet as they come and go and lead my imagination on, and bend it to the desire of that dear shadow! She
is hidden in cambric and in the lace of a skirt flowing on the
ground, floating about heel and toe as if to surround her step
before she takes it, as (with folds thrown back in a train) she
walks forth with her cunning twin arrows.

Has she—herself the walker—a reason for standing there? And
yet have I the right, on my side, to penetrate this mystery further by lifting my head above these reeds and waking from that
deep imaginative drowse in which my clear vision has been
veiled?

"Whatever your features may be, Madame (I whisper to myself), I sense that the instinctive, subtle charm created here by the
sound of my arrival would be broken if I saw them—a charm not
to be denied the explorer by the most exquisitely knotted of

sashes, with its diamond buckle. An image as vague as this is self-sufficient; and it will not destroy the delight which has the stamp of generality, which permits and commands me to forget all real faces; for if I saw one (oh, don't bend yours here, don't let me see it on this ephemeral threshold where I reign supreme!), it would break the spell which is of another world."

I can introduce myself in my pirate dress and say that I happened here by chance.

Separate as we are, we are together. Now I plunge within this mingled intimacy, in this moment of waiting on the water; my revery keeps her here in hesitation, better than visit upon visit could do. How many fruitless talks there would have to be— when I compare them to the one I have had, unheard—before we could find so intimate an understanding as we do now, while I listen along the level of the boat and the expanse of sand now silent!

The waiting moment lasts while I decide.

Oh, my dream, give counsel! What shall I do?

With a glance I shall gather up the virginal absence scattered through this solitude and steal away with it; just as, in memory of a special site, we pick one of those magical, still unopened water-lilies which suddenly spring up there and enclose, in their deep white, a nameless nothingness made of unbroken reveries, of happiness never to be—made of my breathing, now, as it stops for fear that she may show herself. Steal silently away, rowing bit by bit, so that the illusion may not be shattered by the stroke of oars, nor the plashing of the visible foam, unwinding behind me as I flee, reach the feet of any chance walker on the bank, nor bring with it the transparent resemblance of the theft I made of the flower of my mind.

But if, sensing something unusual, she was induced to appear (my Meditative lady, my Haughty, my Cruel, my Gay unknown), so much the worse for that ineffable face which I shall never know! For I executed my plan according to my rules: I pushed off, turned, and then skirted a river wave; and so, like a noble swan's egg fated never to burst forth in flight, I carried off my imaginary trophy, which bursts only with that exquisite absence of self which many a lady loves to pursue in summer along the paths of her park, as she stops sometimes and lingers by a spring which must be crossed or by a lake.

Glory

THE MEANING OF Glory! Just yesterday I learned it! Glory irrefragable! And whatever else henceforth is called by that name cannot affect me.

Endless placards, traitors to literature, drank up the golden daylight which is a mystery to the many and fled back to the very borders of the city; and all the while my eyes, drawn to the horizon's edge as I made my departure on the train, awaited the moment of withdrawal into the mystical pride inspired by a forest whenever we approach it in its time of greatness.

But in the exaltation of that hour the name of Fontainebleau —known for its unfolding of endless, slowly disappearing mountain peaks—was so discordantly, distortedly screeched, that I nearly broke the compartment window and throttled the interrupter. Be still! Or else your thoughtless barking will betray the shadow here which has gently crept within my mind, now that the carriage doors, banging back and forth beneath an inspired and equalitarian wind, have spewed forth their ubiquitous tourists. A faery quietness from rich woods hovers hereabout in some nameless and exceptional state of illusion; and yet you say that these travelers have left the capital to come to your *station!* My good fellow, screeching is your duty. I shan't ask to monopolize that ecstasy which is duly allotted to all citizens through the combined generosities of State and Nature; I ask you only for enough time and silence to let me leave that urban delegation and reach the ecstatic torpor of those leaves. They sit too motionless; soon they must be scattered in the air by the slightest breath. Here, now (I intend no bribery), take this money.

An unresponsive uniform leads me to a gate; and without further ado I give my ticket, rather than my doubtless filthy lucre.

He must certainly have done my bidding, to judge merely by the road as it stretches out in front of me, untrodden. Yet in this glorious, exceptional October, I find it unthinkable that some-one other than myself has not stolen quietly away from those thousands of beings who here display their emptiness and the immense, haunting monotonousness of the capital (their spell will soon be broken when the whistle blows in the mist)—and I cannot imagine that someone has not sensed that there are bitter and luminous sobbings in the air this year, many a vague and drifting thought falling from the boughs of chance, a nameless shuddering in the air, recalling an autumn beneath the heavens.

No, there was no one. The wings of doubt flew up, and I stood like one who has a prize of secret brilliance, a trophy too invaluable to be shown. Nor did I dash immediately into that day watch of immortal trunks bending down to me with superhuman pride (surely we must see their meaning and reality); nor yet did I pass that threshold where, in lofty trust, torches burn all dreams before they can burst forth in purple color in the clouds and sound forth the universal rite of the royal intruder who has only to come. And so, that I might be that prince, I waited until the train, in its slow and then in its regular rhythmical motion, had shrunk to the proportions of a childish monster carrying passengers somewhere—that train which had left me there alone.

ESSAYS

Art for All

WHATEVER IS SACRED, whatever is to remain sacred, must be clothed in mystery. All religions take shelter behind arcana which they unveil only to the predestined. Art has its own mysteries.

We can find an example of this in music. If we open any work of Mozart, Beethoven, or Wagner and glance quickly at the first page, we will be overcome with religious astonishment at the sight of those macabre processions of rigid, chaste, and undeciphered signs. Then we will shut the missal, and it will still remain untouched by any profane thought.

I have often wondered why one art in particular, the greatest of arts, has been refused this necessary characteristic; an art which faces hypocritical curiosity without mystery, blasphemy without terror, and suffers the smiles and grimaces of the ignorant and the hostile.

That art is poetry. *Flowers of Evil,* for example, is printed with the sort of type which burgeons forth every morning in the flower-beds of some utilitarian tirade, and it is sold in black and white books which are exactly the same as those filled with the viscount of Terrail's prose or Mr. Legouvé's poetry.

9

Thus those who are first in line go right into a masterpiece; and ever since the beginning of poetry, no one has kept these intruders away by inventing an immaculate language, a series of sacred formulae which would blind the common eye with dull study, but arouse the patience of the predestined. And to think that the admission ticket of these intruders consists of a page of the alphabet which they have learned to read!

Oh, golden clasps of ancient missals! Oh, immaculate hieroglyphs of papyrus rolls!

What is the result of this absence of mystery?

Poetry, like all things of perfect beauty, is perforce admired. But the admiration is distant, vague—a stupid admiration since it is the mob's. Then, because of this general reaction, a fantastic, preposterous idea occurs to these minds: namely, that poetry must be *taught* in school; and so, like anything else that is taught to the many, poetry is inevitably reduced to the level of a science. It is explained to all alike, democratically. For it is difficult to tell in advance which tousled head contains the white sibylline star.

Therefore, since nobody can be fairly called a complete person if he does not know history (i.e., a science), if he misunderstands physics (i.e., a science), so nobody has received a *solid* education if he cannot *judge* Homer and *read* Hugo (i.e., men of science).

A man (I mean one of those men who has received the empty title of "citizen" from modern vanity, since the latter is hard up for flattering names), a citizen (and this has sometimes made me think, and proudly confess, that music, which is an aroma breathed out by the censer of dreams, is yet different from more palpable aromas in the sense that it brings with it no ecstatic delight), this man, as I was saying, or rather this citizen, strides through our museums with a careless freedom and an absent-minded frigidity which he would not dare exhibit even in a church. For there he would know that he must at least pretend to be interested in some way. From time to time he turns to Rubens and Delacroix with a glance reeking of vulgarity. If we whisper the names of Shakespeare or Goethe as quietly as we can, this character lifts his head as if to say: "That's for me."

The fact is that, since music is an art, since painting is an art, since sculpture is an art in everybody's mind; and since poetry is no longer an art in anybody's mind (and notice that people would be ashamed if they were not *acquainted* with poetry; yet I don't know anyone who has to be ashamed of not being an expert in art), music, painting, and sculpture are therefore left to "those who are in the business," whereas people *learn* poetry because they want to appear educated.

It should be said here that certain awkwardly heroic writers are wrong to call the mob to account for its inept taste and nonexistent imagination. "To insult the mob is to degrade oneself," as Charles Baudelaire rightly observed; and, in any case, the artist should scorn to attack the Philistines. However glorious and saintly the exception may be, he still proves the rule. And who will deny that the rule is the absence of ideal? Then again, it is not only the serenity of scorn that impels us to avoid these recriminations; reason teaches us that they can only be useless or harmful: useless if the Philistine pays no attention to them; harmful if he becomes irritated with the widespread stupidity of the mob, clings to the poets, and thus swells the army of false admirers. I prefer the profane to the profaner. Let us remember that the poet (whether he rhymes, sings, paints, or sculptures) is not on a level beneath which other men crawl; the mob is a level and the poet flies above it. Seriously, has the Bible ever told us that angels mock man because he has no wings?

Men must be made to believe that they can be complete even if they have not read Hugo's poetry, just as they believe that they are complete even if they have not read Verdi's music at sight. The educational bases of the multitude need not include art; that is, a mystery accessible only to the very few. The multitude would profit in that they would no longer waste time dozing over Virgil, and could devote that time to action and to a practical purpose. Poetry, on its side, would profit because it would no longer be irritated (only a slight irritation, it must be admitted, for something which is immortal) by the barking sounds of a pursuing pack of creatures who, simply because they are educated and intelligent, think they have the right to judge it or, even worse, dictate to it.

But, after all, poets, and even the greatest poets, are perfectly acquainted with that difficulty.

In other words, I congratulate any *philosopher* who seeks popularity. He is not supposed to close his hand irrevocably upon the fistful of radiant truths that it holds; he scatters them, and it is proper that each of his fingers should leave them in its luminous wake. But when a *poet,* a worshipper of beauty which is inaccessible to the mob, is not content with the Sanhedrin of art, then I am bothered and I simply don't understand.

Let man be democratic; the artist must separate and remain an aristocrat.

And yet this is precisely what does not happen. Cheap editions of the poets' work are increased with the consent and even the blessing of the poets themselves. Oh, dreamers, oh, singers, do you suppose that this is the way to win glory? When the artist alone possessed your work you had a true admirer, even though he had to spend his last cent for the most recent of your gems. But does this mob understand you now that it has *bought* you because you were cheap? One last barrier—the seven francs it would have to spend—still separated you from the mob's desires (desires already cheapened by teaching), and now you foolishly knock that barrier down! Oh, enemies to yourselves! Why do you encourage (even more through your doctrines than through the price of your books, which is not entirely in your own hands), why do you preach that blasphemy which is the popularization of art? So then, are you going to walk in the company of those who blot out music's mysterious notes (this is not a laughing matter, for the idea has spread everywhere), who unveil its mysteries to the crowd? Or in the company of those who spread it to the countryside, at any price; who care not whether the playing is out of tune, so long as there is playing? What will come of this on some future day, on the day of judgment? You too will be *taught*, like those great martyrs Homer, Lucretius, and Juvenal!

You may say: "What of Corneille, Molière, and Racine? They are popular and glorious." No, they are not popular. Their names are popular, perhaps; but their poetry is not. The mob has read them once, that is true; and without understanding them. But who rereads them? Only artists.

You have already had to pay the penalty: for in the midst of your exquisite and dazzling works you have occasionally scattered verses which lack that high aroma of supreme distinction which usually hovers about them. And *these* are the verses which the mob will admire. You will stand by helplessly and see that your true masterpieces are accessible only to exceptional spirits and neglected by this mob which never should have seen them at all. If this were not already true, if the masses had not already withered his poems, it is certain that the truly radiant works of Hugo would not be *Moses* or *Pray, my child,* as the masses think they are, but *Faun* or *Tears in the night.*

The present hour is a grave one. The people are being educated and great doctrines are going to be spread. If there is a popularization, let us make sure that it is a popularization of the good, not of the beautiful; that your efforts do not tend—and I trust that they have not tended in that direction—to make you a *workers' poet,* which would be grotesque, if it were not pitiful, for the truly superior artist.

Let the masses read works on moral conduct; but please don't let them ruin our poetry.

Oh, poets, you have always been proud; now be more than proud, be scornful!

Autobiography

MY DEAR VERLAINE:

.   .   .   .

Yes, I was born in Paris, March 18, 1842, in the street known today as La Ferrière. Ever since the Revolution, my mother's and father's families had been civil-service employés in Administration or Registry offices; and although they had almost always held good jobs and intended that I follow in their footsteps, I avoided that sort of career. Several of my ancestors, however, apparently used their pens for something other than the signing of bills: one of them (doubtless before the creation of the Registry Office) was an agent for a publishing house under Louis XVI, and I have come across his name at the bottom of the royal Imprimatur for the first French edition of Beckford's *Vathek,* which I have had reissued; another wrote light verse in the *Almanachs des Muses* and *Etrennes aux Dames.* When I was still a child, living within the time-worn circle of my middle-class Parisian family, I met a Mr. Magnien, a third cousin; he had published a wild Romantic book called *Angel* or *Devil* which turns up now and again (high-priced) in the booksellers' catalogues I receive.

I say "Parisian family" because we have always lived in Paris; but the family's origins are Burgundian, Lorrainese, and even Dutch.

When I was a child of seven, I lost my mother, so that I was first brought up by a loving grandmother. Then I went through a number of boarding and secondary schools; my soul was Lamartinian and my secret desire for the future was to take Béranger's place, because I had met him at a friend's house. Apparently that ambition was too complicated ever to be realized; but at any rate I tried for a long time in countless little verse-books which, if I remember correctly, were always taken away from me and destroyed.

As you know, when I was growing up, there was no way for a poet to live by his poetry, even if he moved it down a few pegs. I have never regretted this situation. I learned English simply in order to be able to read Poe better; then, when I was twenty, I went to England, mainly to get away from it all, but also to learn to speak the language and teach it in some quiet little place without having to make money in any other way; I had gotten married and I had to do something pretty quickly.

Today—twenty years later—despite all the time I have had to waste, I feel (with a touch of sadness) that I was right. Because (apart from the prose pieces, the early poems, and the others which echo them in the first issues of various literary reviews) I have always dreamed of, and attempted, something else; patient as an alchemist and ready to sacrifice all vanity and satisfaction to it, just as men used to burn their furniture and the beams of their house to feed the furnace of the Great Work. What work? It is hard to explain. I mean a book, simply; a book in many volumes; a book which *is* a book, architectural and premeditated, and not a miscellany of chance inspirations, however marvelous they may be. I will go even further and say: the Book, for I am convinced that there is only One, and that it has been attempted by every writer, even by Geniuses. The Orphic explanation of the Earth, which is the poet's sole duty and the true function of literature. For the very rhythm of the book, impersonal and alive even in its pagination, would then be juxtaposed to the equations of this dream, this Ode.

There, my dear fellow, you have the confession of my vice—my vice laid bare. I have fought it off a thousand times, wounded or weary at heart; but it possesses me, and perhaps one day I shall succeed. Not that I will accomplish the work in its entirety—it would take a miracle poet to do *that!* But I may be able to reveal and realize a fragment of it, bring its glorious reality to brilliance in some small way, and so suggest the rest of it, which a single life cannot accomplish; I may prove, through the parts I do, that this book exists, and that I was thoroughly acquainted with the parts I could not do.

So that you can easily see why I haven't been in a hurry to collect the countless little bits of poetry which are already known to you and which have occasionally attracted a few well-wishing, fascinating, and excellent minds—yours in particular. That sort of work had only a momentary value for me; it "kept my hand in"; and however successful one or the other of the poems may be, it would hardly be possible to make an album of them, let alone a book. Vanier may be able to snatch some of these bits away from me for publication; but I will simply paste them on pages as one collects certain rags of ageless and therefore precious material. The title, then, might have that condemnatory word "Album" on it—it might be *Album of Verse and Prose,* I am not sure. It will contain several series, and might even go on indefinitely—as distinct from my private work which will, I think, be anonymous, since the Text would speak for itself without its author's voice.

You can find my poems and prose-poems in out-of-print de luxe editions as well as in the literary reviews—works such as my *Vathek,* the *Raven,* or the *Faun.*

Once or twice, when I have been hard up or wanted to buy an old boat, I have had to do textbooks (e.g., *The Ancient Gods, English Words*) which it would be just as well not to mention; but, apart from those, I have not often yielded to necessity or pleasure. At one time, though, I did give up in desperation on that tyrannical book of my dreams; and after I had peddled a few articles here and there, I tried to get out a review by myself called *The Latest Fashion,* and write about dresses, jewels, furniture, even theater programs and dinner menus. The eight or ten numbers which actually appeared still set me to dreaming whenever I get them out and dust them off.

Essentially, I feel that our time is an interregnum for the poet; he should stay out of it; it is at once too obsolete and too seething with preparation; all he can do is work in mystery with an eye to the future or to eternity, and occasionally send his visiting card, a few stanzas, or a sonnet to the "living," so that they won't stone him, should they suspect him of realizing that they do not exist.

Solitude is the necessary condition of such an attitude; and except for the walk from my house (89 Rue de Rome, now) to the various places where my time pays (at first it was the Condorcet and Janson de Sailly schools, then the Collège Rollin), I don't get out much. What I like best is to stay in my apartment, protected by my family, living with a few ancient pieces of furniture which I love, and with a sheet of paper which is often blank. My closest friends have been Villiers and Mendès, and for ten years I used to see my dear friend Manet every day. I can't bring myself to believe that he is no longer with us.

It was your *Accursed Poets,* my dear Verlaine, and Huysmans' *Against the Grain* that drew the young poets to those Tuesday evenings of mine which had long been empty (I am not counting the regular Mallarmeans, of course). What seemed to be my influence on them was really nothing more than a common meeting-ground. I had simply matured quickly enough to get a ten-year head-start in the direction which young minds like mine have since followed.

So that is my whole life, stripped of all the anecdotes which the leading newspapers have been printing *ad nauseam* for so long. They have always thought me very weird. Yes, I think that is all I can find to say, except for the usual daily worries, joys, and inner mourning. I have gone out occasionally whenever there was a ballet to be seen or an organ to be heard: these are my two artistic passions, almost opposite in nature; but their common meaning will some day be brilliantly evident. That, I think, is all. I forgot to add that whenever my mind is too exhausted, I escape to a place on the edge of the Seine and the forest of Fontainebleau which I have been going to for years. There I have a completely different impression of myself; my only passion is sailing on the river—river which I honor, for entire days are swallowed up in its watery abyss without giving us the impression

that we have lost them or leaving even a shadow of remorse. There
I am a simple traveler in my mahogany yawls, or the passionate
sailor proud of his fleet.

    .   .   .   .

Au revoir, my dear fellow.

The Evolution of Literature

(STÉPHANE MALLARMÉ: One of the most generally beloved men of
letters, along with Catulle Mendès. Average height; pointed
beard turning grey; large straight nose; long, pointed ears like
those of a satyr; wide-open eyes of extraordinary brilliance; an
unusual expression of finesse tempered by the appearance of great
goodness. Whenever he speaks, his words are accompanied by
rhythmical gestures full of grace, precision, and eloquence. His
voice drags a little at the end of his words and becomes gradually
gentler. There is great charm in this man. You feel that there is
an incorruptible pride in him which lifts him above all things;
the pride of a god or seer. And once this is felt, inwardly and instinctively you bow down before him).

"We are now witnessing a spectacle," he told me, "which is
truly extraordinary, unique in the history of poetry: every poet
is going off by himself with his own flute, and playing the songs
he pleases. For the first time since the beginning of poetry, poets
have stopped singing bass. Hitherto, as you know, if they wished
to be accompanied, they had to be content with the great organ
of official meter. Well, it was simply overplayed and they got
tired of it! I am sure that when the great Hugo died, he was convinced that he had buried all poetry for the next century; and yet

Paul Verlaine had already written *Sagesse*. We can forgive Hugo his illusion, when we remember all the miracles he produced; he was simply forgetting the eternal instinct, the perpetual and unavoidable growth of the lyrical. But the essential and undeniable point is this: that in a society without stability, without unity, there can be no stable or definitive art. From that incompletely organized society—which also explains the restlessness of certain minds—the unexplained need for individuality was born. The literary manifestations of today are a direct reflection of that need.

"A more immediate explanation of recent innovations is this: it has finally been understood that the old verse form was *not* the absolute, unique, and changeless form, but just one way to be sure of writing good verse. We say to children: 'Don't steal, and you'll be honest.' That is true, but it is not everything. Is it possible to write poetry without reference to time-honored precepts? Poets have answered this question affirmatively, and I believe that they are right. Poetry is everywhere in language, so long as there is rhythm—everywhere except on posters and the back page of the newspaper. In the genre we call 'prose,' there are verses—sometimes admirable verses—of all sorts of rhythms. Actually, there is no such thing as prose: there is the alphabet, and then there are verses which are more or less closely knit, more or less diffuse. So long as there is stylistic effort, there is versification.

"I said a minute ago that today's poetry is, in the main, the result of the poets' boredom with official verse. Even the partisans of official verse share this boredom. Isn't it rather abnormal that, when we open a book of poetry, we should be sure of finding uniform and conventional rhythms throughout? And yet, all the while, the writer hopes to arouse our interest in the essential variety of human feelings! Where is the inspiration in all this! Where is the unforeseen! How tiresome it all is! Official verse must be used only in the crisis moments of the soul. Modern poets have understood this. With a fine sense of the delicate and the sparing, they hover around the official alexandrine, approach it with unusual timidity, almost with fear; and rather than use it as their principle or as a point of departure, they suddenly conjure it up, and with it they crown their poem or period!

"Moreover, the same transformation has taken place in music. Instead of the very clearly delineated melodies of the past, we have an infinity of broken melodies which enrich the poetic texture, and we no longer have the impression of strong cadence."

"Is that how the scission was effected?" I asked.

"Why, yes. The Parnassians were fond of a very formal prosody which has its own beauty, and they failed to realize that the modern poets were simply complementing their work; this also had the advantage of creating a sort of interregnum for the noble alexandrine which had been at bay, crying for mercy. What we have to realize is that the most recent poetical writings do not tend to suppress the official verse; they tend rather to let a little more air into the poem, to create a kind of fluidity or mobility between long-winded verses, which has heretofore been lacking. In an orchestra, for example, you may suddenly hear very fine bursts of sound from the basses; but you know perfectly well that if there were nothing but that, you would soon have enough of it. Young poets space these bursts so that they will occur only when a total effect is to be produced. In this way, the alexandrine (which was invented by nobody, but rather poured forth spontaneously from the instrument of language) will get out of its present finicky, sedentary state, and henceforth it will be freer, more sudden, more refreshed. Its value will lie exclusively in its use during the soul's most serious times. And future volumes of poetry will be traversed by a majestic first verse which scatters in its wake an infinity of motifs originating in the individual's sensibility.

"So there has been scission because both sides have been unaware that their points of view are reconcilable rather than mutually destructive. On the one hand, the Parnassians have, in effect, been perfectly obedient servants of verse, and have sacrificed their personalities. The young poets, on the other hand, have anchored their instinct in a variety of modes, as if there were no precedent; actually, all they are doing is reducing here and there the stiffness of the Parnassian structures; and it seems to me that the two points of view are complementary.

"Despite all this, I still believe, personally, that, with the miraculous knowledge of verse and with the superb instinct for rhythmic pause which such masters as Banville possess, the alexandrine can be infinitely varied and can reproduce all possible shades of human passion. Banville's *Forgeron,* for example, has a number of alexandrines which seem interminable, yet others which are unbelievably concise.

"But, after all, it was a good thing to give our perfect and traditional poetic instrument a little rest. It had been overworked."

"So much for form," I said. "What about content?"

"As far as content is concerned," he answered, "I feel that the young poets are nearer than the Parnassians to the poetic ideal. The latter still treat their subjects as the old philosophers and orators did: that is, they present things directly, whereas I think that they should be presented allusively. Poetry lies in the *contemplation* of things, in the image emanating from the reveries which things arouse in us. The Parnassians take something in its entirety and simply exhibit it; in so doing, they fall short of mystery; they fail to give our minds that exquisite joy which consists of believing that we are creating something. To *name* an object is largely to destroy poetic enjoyment, which comes from gradual divination. The ideal is to *suggest* the object. It is the perfect use of this mystery which constitutes symbol. An object must be gradually evoked in order to show a state of soul; or else, choose an object and from it elicit a state of soul by means of a series of decodings."

"Now," I said, "we are coming to the big objection I was going to make: obscurity!"

"Yes, it is a dangerous thing," he replied, "regardless of whether it results from the reader's inadequacy or from the poet's. But if you avoid the work it involves, you are cheating. If a person of mediocre intelligence and insufficient literary experience hap-

pens to open an obscure book and insists on enjoying it, something is wrong; there has simply been a misunderstanding. There
must always be enigma in poetry. The purpose of literature—the
only purpose—is to *evoke* things."

"Was it you, sir," I asked, "who created the new movement in
poetry?"

"I detest 'schools,' " he replied, "and anything resembling
schools. The professorial attitude toward literature is repugnant
to me. Literature is entirely an individual matter. As far as I am
concerned, a poet today, in the midst of this society which refuses
to let him live, is a man who seeks out solitude in order to sculpture his own tomb. The reason I appear to be the leader of a
school, is, first of all, that I have always taken an interest in the
ideas of young poets; and second, because of my sincerity in
recognizing the originality of what the latest writers have contributed. In reality, I am a hermit. I believe that poetry should
be for the supreme pomp and circumstance of a constituted
society in which glory should have its place. Most people seem
to have forgotten glory. In our time the poet can only go on strike
against society, and turn his back on all the contaminated ways
and means that are offered him. For anything that is offered him
is necessarily inferior to his ideal and to his secret labor."

I then asked Mallarmé what Verlaine's position would be in
the history of this poetic movement.

"He was the first to react against the impeccable and impas-
sible Parnassian attitudes. His fluid verse and certain of his
intentional dissonances were already evident in *Sagesse*. Later
on, around 1875, all the Parnassians (except for a few friends
such as Mendès, Dierx, and Cladel) shrieked with horror at my
Afternoon of a Faun, and, all together, they threw it out. For I
was trying, actually, to make a sort of running pianistic commentary upon the fully preserved and dignified alexandrine—a
sort of musical accompaniment which the poet composes himself, so that the official verse will appear only on the really important occasions. But the father, the real father of all the young
poets is Verlaine, the magnificent Verlaine. The attitude of the

man is just as noble as the attitude of the writer. For it is the only possible attitude at a time when all poets are outlaws. Think of absorbing all the grief that he has—and with his pride and his tremendous pluck!"

"What do you think of the end of Naturalism?"

"Up to now, writers have entertained the childish belief that if they could just choose a certain number of precious stones, for example, and put the names on paper, they would be *making* precious stones. Now, really! that is impossible, no matter how well it is done. Poetry consists of *creation:* we must delve into our souls for states and gleams of such perfect purity, so perfectly sung and illuminated, that they will truly be the jewels of man. When we do that, we have symbol, we have creation, and the word 'poetry' has its full meaning. This, in short, is the only possible human creation. And if, in fact, the precious stones we wear do *not* show a state of soul, they are improperly worn. Take women, for example, eternal thieves that they are. . . .

"And just think," he added, chuckling; "the marvelous thing about jewelry stores is that, occasionally, we learn from the chief of police that what the woman wore improperly was something she didn't know the secret meaning of—something, therefore, which didn't belong to her.

"But to get back to Naturalism. It seems to me that when we use that word, we mean the work of Emile Zola; and when he has finished his work, the name will disappear. I have great admiration for Zola. Actually, what he does is not so much literature as evocative art. He depends as little as possible on literary means. True, he uses words, but that is all. Everything else is based on his marvelous sense of organization and has immediate repercussions in the mind of the mob. His talent is truly powerful; consider his tremendous feeling for life, his mob movements, that texture in Nana's skin that every one of us has touched; and he paints it all with prodigious colors. It really is an admirably organized piece of work. But literature is more of an intellectual thing than that. Things already exist, we don't have to create them; we simply have to see their relationships. It is the threads of those relationships which go to make up poetry and music."

"Are you acquainted with the psychological novel?"

"Slightly. After the great works of Flaubert, the Goncourt brothers, and Zola—which are, in a sense, poems—novelists seem to be going back to the old eighteenth-century French taste which was much more humble and modest, consisting, as it did, not of a pictorial presentation of the outer form of things but rather of a dissection of the motives of the human soul. But there is the same difference between that and poetry as there is between a corset and a beautiful throat."

Before leaving, I asked Mallarmé for the names of those who seemed to him to represent the modern evolution in poetry.

"The young poets," he answered, "who seem to me to have done truly masterful work—that is, original work, completely divorced from the past—are: Morice, Moréas (a delightful poet), and, above all, the man who has given poetry the biggest boost, Henri de Régnier. Like de Vigny, he lives apart, at some distance from here, in retreat and silence. I greatly respect and admire him. His latest work, *Poèmes anciens et romanesques,* is a pure masterpiece.

"So you can see," he said, shaking hands with me, "that, in the final analysis, all earthly existence must ultimately be contained in a book."

The Book: A Spiritual Instrument

I AM THE AUTHOR of a statement to which there have been varying reactions, including praise and blame, and which I shall make again in the present article. Briefly, it is this: all earthly existence must ultimately be contained in a book.

It terrifies me to think of the qualities (among them genius,

certainly) which the author of such a work will have to possess.
I am one of the unpossessed. We will let that pass and imagine
that it bears no author's name. What, then, will the work itself
be? I answer: a hymn, all harmony and joy; an immaculate
grouping of universal relationships come together for some
miraculous and glittering occasion. Man's duty is to observe with
the eyes of the divinity; for if his connection with that divinity
is to be made clear, it can be expressed only by the pages of the
open book in front of him.

Seated on a garden bench where a recent book is lying, I like
to watch a passing gust half open it and breathe life into many
of its outer aspects, which are so obvious that no one in the history of literature has ever thought about them. I shall have the
chance to do so now, if I can get rid of my overpowering newspaper. I push it aside; it flies about and lands near some roses
as if to hush their proud and feverish whispering; finally, it un-
folds around them. I will leave it there along with the silent
whispering of the flowers. I formally propose now to examine
the differences between this rag and the book, which is supreme.
The newspaper is the sea; literature flows into it at will.

Now then—

The foldings of a book, in comparison with the large-sized,
open newspaper, have an almost religious significance. But an
even greater significance lies in their thickness when they are
piled together; for then they form a tomb in miniature for our
souls.

Every discovery made by printers has hitherto been absorbed
in the most elementary fashion by the newspaper, and can be
summed up in the word: Press. The result has been simply a
plain sheet of paper upon which a flow of words is printed in the
most unrefined manner. The immediacy of this system (which
preceded the production of books) has undeniable advantages
for the writer; with its endless line of posters and proof sheets
it makes for improvisation. We have, in other words, a "daily
paper." But who, then, can make the gradual discovery of the
meaning of this format, or even of a sort of popular fairyland

charm about it? Then again, the leader, which is the most important part, makes its great free way through a thousand obstacles and finally reaches a state of disinterestedness. But what is the result of this victory? It overthrows the advertisement (which is Original Slavery) and, as if it were itself the powered printing press, drives it far back beyond intervening articles onto the fourth page and leaves it there in a mass of incoherent and inarticulate cries. A noble spectacle, without question. After this, what else can the newspaper possibly need in order to overthrow the *book* (even though at the bottom—or rather at its foundation, i.e., the *feuilleton*—it resembles the other in its pagination, thus generally regulating the columns)? It will need nothing, in fact; or practically nothing, if the book delays as it is now doing and carelessly continues to be a drain for it. And since even the book's format is useless, of what avail is that extraordinary addition of foldings (like wings in repose, ready to fly forth again) which constitute its rhythm and the chief reason for the secret contained in its pages? Of what avail the priceless silence living there, and evocative symbols following in its wake, to delight the mind which literature has totally delivered?

Yes, were it not for the folding of the paper and the depths thereby established, that darkness scattered about in the form of black characters could not rise and issue forth in gleams of mystery from the page to which we are about to turn.

The newspaper with its full sheet on display makes improper use of printing—that is, it makes good packing paper. Of course, the obvious and vulgar advantage of it, as everybody knows, lies in its mass production and circulation. But that advantage is secondary to a miracle, in the highest sense of the word: words led back to their origin, which is the twenty-four letters of the alphabet, so gifted with infinity that they will finally consecrate Language. Everything is caught up in their endless variations and then rises out of them in the form of the Principle. Thus typography becomes a rite.

The book, which is a total expansion of the letter, must find its mobility in the letter; and in its spaciousness must establish some nameless system of relationships which will embrace and strengthen fiction.

There is nothing fortuitous in all this, even though ideas may seem to be the slaves of chance. The system guarantees them. Therefore we must pay no attention to the book industry with its materialistic considerations. The making of a book, with respect to its flowering totality, begins with the first sentence. From time immemorial the poet has knowingly placed his verse in the sonnet which he writes upon our minds or upon pure space. We, in turn, will misunderstand the true meaning of this book and the miracle inherent in its structure, if we do not knowingly imagine that a given motif has been properly placed at a certain height on the page, according to its own or to the book's distribution of light. Let us have no more of those successive, incessant, back and forth motions of our eyes, traveling from one line to the next and beginning all over again. Otherwise we will miss that ecstasy in which we become immortal for a brief hour, free of all reality, and raise our obsessions to the level of creation. If we do not actively create in this way (as we would music on the keyboard, turning the pages of a score), we would do better to shut our eyes and dream. I am not asking for any servile obedience. For, on the contrary, each of us has within him that lightning-like initiative which can link the scattered notes together.

Thus, in reading, a lonely, quiet concert is given for our minds, and they in turn, less noisily, reach its meaning. All our mental faculties will be present in this symphonic exaltation; but, unlike music, they will be rarefied, for they partake of thought. Poetry, accompanied by the Idea, is perfect Music, and cannot be anything else.

Now, returning to the case at hand and to the question of books which are read in the ordinary way, I raise my knife in protest, like the cook chopping off chickens' heads.

The virginal foldings of the book are unfortunately exposed to the kind of sacrifice which caused the crimson-edged tomes of ancient times to bleed. I mean that they invite the paper-knife,

which stakes out claims to possession of the book. Yet our consciousness alone gives us a far more intimate possession than
such a barbarian symbol; for it joins the book now here, now
there, varies its melodies, guesses its riddles, and even re-creates
it unaided. The folds will have a mark which remains intact and
invites us to open or close the pages according to the author's
desires. There can be only blindness and discourtesy in so mur-
derous and self-destructive an attempt to destroy the fragile, in-
violable book. The newspaper holds the advantage here, for it is
not exposed to such treatment. But it is nonetheless an annoying
influence; for upon the book—upon the divine and intricate
organism required by literature—it inflicts the monotonousness
of its eternally unbearable columns, which are merely strung
down the pages by hundreds.

"But,"

I hear some one say, "how can this situation be changed?" I
shall take space here to answer this question in detail; for the
work of art—which is unique or should be—must provide illustrations. A tremendous burst of greatness, of thought, or of emotion, contained in a sentence printed in large type, with one
gradually descending line to a page, should keep the reader
breathless throughout the book and summon forth his powers
of excitement. Around this would be smaller groups of secondary
importance, commenting on the main sentence or derived from
it, like a scattering of ornaments.

It will be said, I suppose, that I am attempting to flabbergast
the mob with a lofty statement. That is true. But several of my
close friends must have noticed that there are connections between this and their own instinct for arranging their writings
in an unusual and ornamental fashion, halfway between verse
and prose. Shall I be explicit? All right, then, just to maintain
that reputation for clarity so avidly pursued by our make-
everything-clear-and-easy era. Let us suppose that a given writer
reveals one of his ideas in theoretical fashion and, quite possibly,
in useless fashion, since he is ahead of his time. He well knows
that such revelations, touching as they do on literature, should

be brought out in the open. And yet he hesitates to divulge too brusquely things which do not yet exist; and thus, in his modesty, and to the mob's amazement, he veils them over.

It is because of those daydreams we have before we resume our reading in a garden that our attention strays to a white butterfly flitting here and there, then disappearing; but also leaving behind it the same slight touch of sharpness and frankness with which I have presented these ideas, and flying incessantly back and forth before the people, who stand amazed.

Mystery in Literature

ANY AFFIRMATIONS I make here, no matter how justified, are naturally going to be cannon fodder for the jokers in the mob.

Every work of art, apart from its inner treasure, should provide some sort of outward—or even indifferent—meaning through its words. A certain deference should be shown the people: for, after all, they *are* lending out their language, and the work is going to turn it to some unexpected account. It is just as well to keep idlers away; they are glad to see that the work does not apply to them—such, at least, is their first impression.

Each to his own way and no hard feelings.

And yet somehow there is a disquieting gleam from the depths of the work, hardly distinguishable from its outward show. The clever idlers become suspicious and tell us to stop; for in their considered opinion the meaning of the work is unintelligible.

Heaven help the poor slandered poet who happens to be involved! He will be crushed beneath an immense and rather silly joke. It has always been so; and now, more than ever before, the unanimous and excessive pestilence rages.

There is certainly something occult in men's hearts; I am convinced that there is something abstruse, something closed and hidden in the Mob. For whenever She sniffs out the idea that obscurity may be a *reality;* that it may exist, for example, on a piece of paper, in a piece of writing (heaven forbid, of course, that it should exist within itself!), She rises up in a hurricane fury and, with thunders and lightnings, blames the darkness on anything but Herself.

Her credulousness finds satisfaction in the corresponding agitations of Her fellow citizens; She jumps to extremes. So that whatever that Dark Fiend from Hell (i.e., the poet) may write henceforth, She will shake Her head (quite unaware that She Herself is the enigma) and, with a whisk of Her skirt, assert: "I don't get it!"—even if the poor poet has simply stated that he is blowing his nose.

Obedient as he is to his inborn rhythmical sense, the poet naturally finds a lack of proportion between the storm's cause and effect.

Those fellow citizens, it seems to him, are wrong; following their avowed intention, they plunge their pens within a Nightless well and lay only the useless, minimum foundation of intelligibility. Granted that the poet does this too—but that is not all he does. It is hardly discreet of them to rouse the Mob to such a fury—the Mob, remember! is the vessel of Genius—and to pour forth pellmell the monumental stupidity of man.

And all this for a matter of no importance.

They play the game without rules and for useless stakes; they force Our Lady and Patron Saint to reveal Her dehiscence, Her lacuna, Her misunderstanding of special dreams which constitute the common measure of all things.

I know for a fact that they are the ones who rush on stage and parade around in humiliating fashion. For to base their arguments on obscurity, to say that they "don't get it" and that if they "don't get it" nobody will, means that they refuse to discriminate from the very outset.

The scandal is typical, and it continues to be irrelevant.

It has to do with an undertaking which is of no literary importance—

Their undertaking—

Which consists of revealing only the monotonous outward aspects of the world, as news-boys do. Admittedly, they are struggling beneath the pressure of the moment; but in that situation it is clearly improper to write at all, save to spread banality abroad. What they fail to spread is the priceless mist that floats about the secret abyss of every human thought. All that is vulgar which receives no more than the stamp of immediacy. And although I hesitate to use an image to "put them in their place" personally, nevertheless the crudity of these bores is such that they give us, I would say, not a labyrinth lit by flowers and beckoning to our leisure, but a road lined with headaches and vertical plaster images of man's interminable blindness, with no hidden fountains or greenery bending above them, but only green bottle bottoms and bristling broken glass.

Even the advertisers shy away from it all.

Now, let us imagine a steady brilliance which, even when intermittent, does not seem to be merely momentary.

Music came along and put an end to that kind of work.

For at some point in the composition, a motif breaks through the musical veils of our imagination and frees itself of their unceasing immobility, which is alternately compacted or dissolved through conscious art.

Such is the ordinary way.

Or else the composition can begin with a triumphant burst of sound too sudden to last; then the surprise dies away in a group of hesitating notes which its echo has liberated.

Then again, there is the reverse order: the hesitations are folded darkly together and rumor forth a particular obsession of the mind; they are crowded and massed together; and then out of them arises an ultimate and essential brilliance.

Such is the twin, intellectual fashion found particularly in symphonies which, in turn, found it in the repertory of nature and of the sky.

Yes, I know; Mystery is said to be Music's domain. But the written word also lays claim to it.

Yes, the supreme and heart-rending musical moments are born of fleeting arabesques, and their bursting is more true, more central, more brilliant than any reasoning. When we consider their matchless efficacy, we feel unable to translate them into any language save that of the listener's ideas. Their contact with our spirit is direct and fitting; we feel somehow that words would be discordant and unwelcome.

And yet the written word, which is the Ideal in noiseless flight from earth, regains its rights as it stands beneath that fall of virginal sounds. Both Music and Lyric call for the previous discarding of the spoken word, of course, in order to prevent mere talking.

In a single surge of opposites, the one descends, the other flies away, and yet the same silken veils follow in the wake of both.

Let me pause now and quietly add this parenthesis. It has always been my purpose that stylistic coloring should be neutral: neither should it be darkened in a dive nor brightly shimmer or splash; nor subject to the alternative, which is rules.

What sure guide is there to intelligibility in the midst of these contrasts? What guarantee?

Syntax.

I do not mean simply such spontaneous twists as are inherent in the facility of conversation, even though they are essential to oratory. The French language in particular is elegant when it appears in negligee. As history will show, this is one of the original French characteristics, one of the nation's truly exquisite natures. But our literature goes beyond this "fashion"; it does not consist merely of correspondence and memoirs. It has its quick high flutterings as well; and when these are on the wing, the writer can observe how extraordinarily well the limpid structure of the language receives the primitive thunderbolts of Logic. The sentence may seem to stammer at first, hold back in a knot of incidental bits; then it multiplies, takes on order, and rises up in a noble harmony, wavering all the while in its knowing transpositions.

For those who may be surprised and angered by the broad application of my words, I shall describe the revels of this Language.

Words rise up unaided and in ecstasy; many a facet reveals its infinite rarity and is precious to our mind. For our mind is the center of this hesitancy and oscillation; it sees the words not in their usual order, but in projection (like the walls of a cave), so long as that mobility which is their principle lives on, that part of speech which is not spoken. Then quickly, before they die away, they all exchange their brilliancies from afar; or they may touch, and steal a furtive glance.

The argument that a certain indispensable and pedestrian clarity may be lacking here and there is a matter for grammarians. And even if the poor reader were to misread these words continually, his understanding of the slush which makes up the current literary fashion is not much better, and so there is hardly any need to distinguish him from the truly malicious. For he too speaks angrily and insultingly of obscurity. Yet why does he not consider literature's common stock and speak angrily and insultingly of *its* incoherence, its drivel, its plagiarism (not to mention any other deterrent or special accusation); or, again, he might well speak of its platitudes, with particular reference to those who are the first to cry "obscurity!" in order to avoid taxing the public's brains.

To answer these threats, I shall simply observe that several of my contemporaries don't know how to read.

The newspaper, yes; they can read that; it has the advantage of not interrupting the day's routine.

Reading—

Is an exercise—

We must bend our independent minds, page by page, to the blank space which begins each one; we must forget the title, for it is too resounding. Then, in the tiniest and most scattered stopping-points upon the page, when the lines of chance have been vanquished word by word, the blanks unfailingly return; before, they were gratuitous; now they are essential; and now at last it is clear that nothing lies beyond; now silence is genuine and just.

It is a virgin space, face to face with the lucidity of our matching vision, divided of itself, in solitude, into halves of whiteness; and each of these is lawful bride to the other at the wedding of the Idea.

Thus the invisible air, or song, beneath the words leads our divining eye from word to music; and thus, like a motif, invisibly it inscribes its fleuron and pendant there.

Crisis in Poetry

A FUNDAMENTAL AND FASCINATING CRISIS in literature is now at hand.

Such is the plain and present truth in the eyes of all those for whom literature is of primary importance. What we are witnessing as the finale of our own century is not upheaval (as was the case a hundred years ago), but rather a fluttering in the temple's veil—meaningful folds and even a little tearing.

This is disconcerting for the French reading public, whose habits were interrupted by the death of Victor Hugo. Pursuing his mysterious task, Hugo reduced all prose—philosophy, oratory, history—to poetry; and since he was himself poetry personified, he nearly abolished the philosopher's, speaker's, or historian's right to self-expression. In that wasteland, with silence all around, he was a monument. Yet in a crypt of equal silence lay the divinity of this majestic, unconscious idea: namely, that the form we call verse is itself, quite simply, literature; that we have verse so long as we have diction, rhythm so long as we have style. Poetry, I think, waited patiently and respectfully until this giant (whose ever more grasping, ever firmer blacksmith's hand was coming to be the definition of verse) had disappeared; then it broke up. The entire language was fitted out for prosody, and therein it re-discovered its vital sense of pause. Now it could fly off, freely scattering its numberless and irreducible elements. Or we might well compare it to the multiple sounds issuing from a purely verbal orchestration.

That was the beginning of the change in poetry which Verlaine, with his fluid verse, had secretly and unexpectedly prepared when he returned to certain primitive resources in language.

I was witness to this adventure. And although my role in it was not so influential as has been claimed (for no single person was responsible), I did at least take great interest in it. It is time to discuss it, and it seems better to do so at a distance, or, so to speak, anonymously.

It will be agreed that because of the priority on magic power which is given to rhyme, French poetry has been intermittent ever since its evolution. It shines for a moment, dies out, and waits. There is extinction—or rather wear and tear which reveal the weft; there is repetition. After an almost century-long period of poetic orgy and excess which can be compared only to the Renaissance, the latest poetic urge (counteracting a number of different circumstances) is being fulfilled not by a darkening or cooling off process, but, on the contrary, by a variation in continuing brilliance. The retempering of verse, ordinarily a secret affair, is now being done openly: poets are resorting to delightful approximations.

The kind of treatment that has been given to the hieratic canon of verse can, I think, be divided into three graduated parts.

Official prosody has cut and dried rules; there lies its obstinacy. It gives its official approval to such "wise" procedures as the observance of the hemistich, and pronounces judgment on the slightest effort to simulate versification. It is like the law which states, for example, that abstinence from theft is the essence of honesty. But this is precisely what we need least to learn; for

if we have not understood it by ourselves from the first, it is useless to obey it.

Those who are still faithful to the alexandrine, i.e., to the
modern hexameter, have gone inside it and loosened this rigid,
childish metrical mechanism; and so, now that such artificial
metronomes have been abolished, there is joy for our ears alone
in perceiving all possible combinations and interrelationships
of twelve tones.

Consider the most recent literary taste.

Here is a rather typical and interesting example of it.

Henri de Régnier, a poet of great tact, still considers the alexandrine to be *the* gem—a gem, however, which (like sword or
flower) he discloses but rarely, and even then only with some well-
considered pattern in mind. He disturbs this verse form only
with the greatest circumspection; he hovers and plays around
it, yields to its related harmonies, and finally shows it forth in all
its pride and purity. His fingering may fail at the eleventh syllable, or often linger on to a thirteenth. He excels in such ac-
companiments, which are, of course, the delicate, proud invention of his own original talent; they point up the temporary
uneasiness of those who play the traditional poetic instrument.
We discover a quite different example of knowing disobedience
in the case of Jules Laforgue, who, in the beginning, abandoned
the old worn-out form and initiated us in the secret and unfailing
charm of defective verse.

Up to now, therefore (as shown in the two examples just mentioned), there has been either the delicacy of a Régnier or the
self-indulgence of a Laforgue in metrical treatment, as a result of
the fatigue brought on by the abuse of our national rhythm. That
rhythm, like the national flag, must be used sparingly. There
has, however, been one interesting exception: an occasional and
wilful disobedience in the form of beautifully executed dissonances for the sensitive ear. And to think that, scarcely fifteen
years ago, pedants that we are, we would have been outraged by
this phenomenon—as if it were an illiterate's sacrilege! Let me

say, finally, that the official alexandrine, like a memory, haunts
about these rhythmic variations and thus adds to their luster.

Modern free verse—unlike the seventeenth-century free verse,
which we find in fables or operas, and which was simply an ar-
rangement of various well-known meters ungoverned by strophes
—derives its entire originality from what we may properly call
its "polymorphic" character. And the breaking up of official verse
should now be what the poets will, should even be endless, provided there is pleasure to be had in it. For example, there might
be a certain euphony which the reader's own poetic instinct could
fragmentize with a sort of native and unerring accuracy (such
has been the recent verse of Moréas). Or perhaps a rhythmical
gesture of languor and revery, or of startled passion (as in the
work of Vielé-Griffin). Prior to these, there was Kahn's very skill-
ful notation of the tonal value of words. But these are only a
few of the names; there are others equally typical; Charles
Morice, Verhaeren, Dujardin, Mockel, etc., whose works should
be consulted; they will bear out what I have said.

But the truly remarkable fact is this: for the first time in the
literary history of any nation, along with the general and traditional great organ of orthodox verse which finds its ecstasy on an
ever-ready keyboard, any poet with an individual technique and
ear can build his own instrument, so long as his fluting, bowing,
or drumming are accomplished—play that instrument and dedi-
cate it, along with others, to Language.

Thus we have won a great new freedom; and it is my firm belief that no beauty of the past has been destroyed as a result. I am
convinced that the solemn poetic tradition which was mainly
established by our classical genius will continue to be observed
on all important occasions. But whenever it shall seem unfitting
to disturb the echoes of that venerable past for sentimental or
narrative purposes, we shall be careful to avoid such disturb-
ance. Each soul is a melody; its strands must be bound up. Each
poet has his flute or viol, with which to do so.

In my opinion, we have been late in finding the true condition and possibility not only of poetic self-expression, but of free and individual modulation.

Languages are imperfect because multiple; the supreme language is missing. Inasmuch as thought consists of writing without pen and paper, without whispering even, without the sound of the immortal Word, the diversity of languages on earth means that no one can utter words which would bear the miraculous stamp of Truth Herself Incarnate. This is clearly nature's law— we stumble on it with a smile of resignation—to the effect that we have no sufficient reason for equating ourselves with God. But then, esthetically, I am disappointed when I consider how impossible it is for language to express things by means of certain keys which would reproduce their brilliance and aura—keys which do exist as a part of the instrument of the human voice, or among languages, or sometimes even in one language. When compared to the opacity of the word *ombre,* the word *ténèbres* does not seem very dark; and how frustrating the perverseness and contradiction which lend dark tones to *jour,* bright tones to *nuit!* We dream of words brilliant at once in meaning and sound, or darkening in meaning and so in sound, luminously and elementally self-succeeding. *But,* let us remember that if our dream were fulfilled, *verse would not exist*—verse which, in all its wisdom, atones for the sins of languages, comes nobly to their aid.

Strange mystery—and so, equally mysterious and meaningful, prosody sprang forth in primitive times.

The ideal would be a reasonable number of words stretched beneath our mastering glance, arranged in enduring figures, and followed by silence.

Granted that individual inventiveness, in the case of a French poet, need not outweigh the influence of his poetic heritage; still it would be highly annoying if he were not able to follow his own paths, walk through their numberless little flowers, and gather up whatever notes his voice might find. The attempt to do so has been made just recently, and poets are still conducting learned research in the direction of syllable stressing, for example. But apart from that, there is the fascinating pastime of break-

ing the old alexandrine into still recognizable fragments, alternately elusive or revealing. This is preferable to total and sudden
novelty. It was good to relax the rules, but the ardor which got
the new school too far out of tune should now be cooled. Most
delightfully out of tune, yes; but to go further, as a result of that
liberation, and to suppose that every poet henceforth should in-
vent his own prosody and base it on his own special musical gift
—to say nothing of his own spelling system—is simply ridiculous.
That kind of thing is cannon fodder for the newspaper boys.
Verses will always be similar, and the old proportions and regu-
larity will be observed, because the poetic act consists of our sudden realization that an idea is naturally fractionized into several
motifs of equal value which must be assembled. They rhyme;
and their outward stamp of authenticity is that common meter
which the final stress establishes.

But the crisis in poetry lies less in the very interesting interregnum or rest treatment undergone by versification, than in
certain new states of our poetic mind.

We now *hear* undeniable rays of light, like arrows gilding and
piercing the meanderings of song. I mean that, since Wagner appeared, Music and Verse have combined to form Poetry.

Either one of these two elements, of course, may profitably
stand apart in triumph and integrity, in a quiet concert of its own
if it chooses not to speak distinctly. Or else the poem can tell of
their reassociation and restrengthening: the instrumentation is
brightened to the point of perfect clarity beneath the orchestral
veil, while verse flies down into the evening darkness of the
sounds. That modern meteor—the symphony—approaches
thought with the consent or ignorance of the musician. And
thought itself is no longer expressed merely in common language.

Thus Mystery bursts forth ineffably throughout the heavens of
Its own impersonal magnificence, wherein it was ordained that
the orchestra should complement our age-old effort to make the
spoken word our only form of music.

Twin symbols interrelated.

The Decadent or Mystic Schools (as they call themselves or

as they were hastily labeled by the public press) find their common meeting-ground in an Idealism which (as in the case of fugues and sonatas) shuns the materials in nature, avoids any thought that might tend to arrange them too directly or precisely, and retains only the suggestiveness of things. The poet must establish a careful relationship between two images, from which a third element, clear and fusible, will be distilled and caught by our imagination. We renounce that erroneous esthetic (even though it has been responsible for certain masterpieces) which would have the poet fill the delicate pages of his book with the actual and palpable wood of trees, rather than with the forest's shuddering or the silent scattering of thunder through the foliage. A few well-chosen sounds blown heavenward on the trumpet of true majesty will suffice to conjure up the architecture of the ideal and only habitable palace—palace of no palpable stone, else the book could not be properly closed.

It is not *description* which can unveil the efficacy and beauty of monuments, seas, or the human face in all their maturity and native state, but rather evocation, *allusion, suggestion*. These somewhat arbitrary terms reveal what may well be a very decisive tendency in modern literature, a tendency which limits literature and yet sets it free. For what is the magic charm of art, if not this: that, beyond the confines of a fistful of dust or of all other reality, beyond the book itself, beyond the very text, it delivers up that volatile scattering which we call the Spirit, Who cares for nothing save universal musicality.

Speech is no more than a commercial approach to reality. In literature, allusion is sufficient: essences are distilled and then embodied in Idea.

Song, when it becomes impalpable joy, will rise to heaven.

This is the ideal I would call Transposition; Structure is something else.

If the poem is to be pure, the poet's voice must be stilled and the initiative taken by the words themselves, which will be set in motion as they meet unequally in collision. And in an exchange of gleams they will flame out like some glittering swath of fire sweeping over precious stones, and thus replace the audible breathing in lyric poetry of old—replace the poet's own personal and passionate control of verse.

The inner structures of a book of verse must be inborn; in this way, chance will be totally eliminated and the poet will be absent. From each theme, itself predestined, a given harmony will be born somewhere in the parts of the total poem and take its proper place within the volume; because, for every sound, there is an echo. Motifs of like pattern will move in balance from point to point. There will be none of the sublime incoherence found in the page-settings of the Romantics, none of the artificial unity that used to be based on the square measurements of the book. Everything will be hesitation, disposition of parts, their alternations and relationships—all this contributing to the rhythmic totality, which will be the very silence of the poem, in its blank spaces, as that silence is translated by each structural element in its own way. (Certain recent publications have heralded this sort of book; and if we may admit their ideals as complements to our own, it must then be granted that young poets have seen what an overwhelming and harmonious totality a poem must be, and have stammered out the magic concept of the Great Work.) Then again, the perfect symmetry of verses within the poem, of poems within the volume, will extend even beyond the volume itself; and this will be the creation of many poets who will inscribe, on spiritual space, the expanded signature of genius —as anonymous and perfect as a work of art.

Chimaera, yes! And yet the mere thought of it is proof (reflected from Her scales) that during the last twenty-five years poetry has been visited by some nameless and absolute flash of lightning—like the muddied, dripping gleams on my window-pane which are washed away and brightened by streaming showers of rain—revealing that, in general, all books contain the amalgamation of a certain number of age-old truths; that actually there is only one book on earth, that it is the law of the earth, the earth's true Bible. The difference between individual works is simply the difference between individual interpretations of one true and established text, which are proposed in a mighty gathering of those ages we call civilized or literary.

Certainly, whenever I sit at concerts, amid the obscurity and ecstasy of sound, I always perceive the nascent form of some one of those poems which have their origin and dwelling in human life—a poem more understandable because unheard, because the composer, in his desire to portray its majestic lines, was not even *tempted* to "explain everything." My feeling—or my doubtlessly ineradicable prejudice as a writer—is that nothing will endure if it remains unspoken; that our present task, precisely (now that the great literary rhythms I spoke of are being broken up and scattered in a series of distinct and almost orchestrated shiverings), is to find a way of transposing the symphony to the Book: in short, to regain our rightful due. For, undeniably, the true source of Music must not be the elemental sound of brasses, strings, or wood winds, but the intellectual and written word in all its glory—Music of perfect fulness and clarity, the totality of universal relationships.

One of the undeniable ideals of our time is to divide words into two different categories: first, for vulgar or immediate, second, for essential purposes.

The first is for narrative, instruction, or description (even though an adequate exchange of human thoughts might well be achieved through the silent exchange of money). The elementary use of language involves that universal *journalistic style* which characterizes all kinds of contemporary writing, with the exception of literature.

Why should we perform the miracle by which a natural object is almost made to disappear beneath the magic waving wand of the written word, if not to divorce that object from the direct and the palpable, and so conjure up its *essence* in all purity?

When I say: "a flower!" then from that forgetfulness to which my voice consigns all floral form, something different from the usual calyces arises, something all music, essence, and softness: the flower which is absent from all bouquets.

Language, in the hands of the mob, leads to the same facility and directness as does money. But, in the Poet's hands, it is turned, above all, to dream and song; and, by the constituent virtue and necessity of an art which lives on fiction, it achieves its full efficacy.

Out of a number of words, poetry fashions a single new word which is total in itself and foreign to the language—a kind of incantation. Thus the desired isolation of language is effected; and chance (which might still have governed these elements, despite their artful and alternating renewal through meaning and sound) is thereby instantly and thoroughly abolished. Then we realize, to our amazement, that we had never truly heard this or that ordinary poetic fragment; and, at the same time, our recollection of the object thus conjured up bathes in a totally new atmosphere.

Music and Literature

LADIES AND GENTLEMEN:

For a long time now, two nations alone—England and France —have shown a common faith in the possibility of Literature. Each has extended or withdrawn the torch, and thus the mutual influence has been brightened. But my main topic and objective this evening is not so much this interchange (although it is partly on that account that I am with you now and speaking to you in my native tongue) as, first of all, the very particular desire for continuity of masterpieces. In no sense can genius fail to be exceptional. Like the jutting corner of a façade, it reaches unexpected heights; yet it does not create vast wild spaces (here, again, it is exceptional), nor does it know abandon, but rather maintains a sort of grouping, an admirable assemblage of lesser, miniature shrines, colonnades, fountains—keeps them as spiritual sites and so produces in perspective a special and continuous palace whose doors are thrown open to the princely instincts in each of us. Thus national taste is born and, in the case of France and England, we linger in our pleasure over the choice between these rival architectures both similar and sublime.

I have been invited on your behalf to speak in some detail of our present literary situation. The time is especially appropriate. For I bring news—the most amazing and unprecedented news. We have been experimenting with verse.

Governments change; prosody remains ever intact; perhaps because during revolutions it goes unnoticed or because attack is not called for upon a dogma considered incapable of change.

There should be no delay in discussing this subject (think of the breathless guest, fresh from his travels, who has been witness to an extraordinary event; he will have no peace until he has poured forth his story). For verse is everything, from the moment we take pen in hand. As long as there is cadence, there will be style and versification. That is why the careful prose of discriminating writers—ornamental prose—can always be thought of as broken verse; it plays with its own tones and hidden rhymes, like a thyrsus of infinite complexity. Such is the flowering of what we have come to call the *prose-poem.*

Meanwhile, the ancient and regular verse stands by with its very strict, numerical, and simple nature.

There can be no doubt that we have now reached the point of separation between the two.

At the beginning of this century, the keen and powerful poetic instinct of the Romantics combined these elements and created flowing alexandrines with regular pauses and run-on lines. Now, however, the combination is breaking up into two separate wholes. Our recent search has apparently been brought to a close by the fortunate discovery of *free verse,* which I like to call an individual modulation; for every soul is a knot of rhythm.

The inevitable result was disagreement. Naturally, certain of the pioneering spirits ventured far afield and thought they had done with what we must call "official" verse. They had not, however; for it will be used on special occasions; their attempt at divorce was overbold, but it was the only one and it will be tempered.

Those who looked askance at the whole affair probably think it was a waste of time.

On the contrary.

For authentic works of art were born, quite apart from the fight over form; and even if their value goes unrecognized, let us prize the special silence which will take their place and thus provide much-needed rest for the ancient instrument of our music. On special occasions verse will always thunder. Yet it should be exceptional, despite the fact that all measured writing, as we have just observed, *is* verse by definition. Similarly, Literature should continue to be the rarest of phenomena, despite our common desire to perpetuate it throughout the ages. French verse in particular is a delicate instrument and should be used sparingly. But now, after the recent interval of silence and hesitation, eternal verse may once again rise up with all its perfect tonalities and flow renewed—rise, accompanied by its newest elements, to the sublime.

Here, then, was a purifying storm; and it is entirely to the credit of the recent generation that, in the midst of all confusion, the act of writing was studied through to its very origin. The greatest progress was made in their answer to a question which I should ask quite simply in the following way: is there a reason for writing at all? It is not *description* which can unveil the efficacy and beauty of monuments, seas, or the human face in all their maturity and native state, but rather *evocation, allusion, suggestion*. These somewhat arbitrary terms reveal what may well be a very decisive tendency in modern literature, a tendency which limits literature and yet sets it free. For what is the magic charm of art, if not this: that, beyond the confines of a fistful of dust or of all other reality, beyond the book itself, beyond the very text, it delivers up that volatile scattering which we call the Spirit, Who cares for nothing save universal musicality.

So now you are up to date on the most recent poetic "fever," its sudden jumps and noble hesitations.

But we cannot let it go at that; for surely I have come here to speak to you of something far greater than the mere renewal of rites and rhymes—something which I scarcely grasp myself; indeed, we may finally *fail* to grasp it; but let us hope at least to touch upon it. You bid me in your kindness to discuss my favorite theme; and fully realizing, as I do, your expectations, I am revisited by that vague desire of bygone days (which, in my solitude, I could never fulfill) to devote some special evening to an all-embracing discovery (from the heavens to the abyss) of that struggle with the Ideal which certain of my contemporaries are now waging—as others struggle with social problems, for example. And so, without further ado, let me ask a question which may seem startling to an audience long since devoted to literary elegance: does Literature exist? Exist in some form other than that convention of classical periods which was the art of etching and refining ideas in all fields? It is axiomatic that in order to perfect the building or the discovery, an architect, a jurist, or a doctor must finally raise them to the level of discourse. In short, everything which emanates from the human mind must be reintegrated. The subject is generally immaterial.

Very few people have faced up to this problem which looms large only late in life. I too have been tardy, and now I suddenly hesitate, when I should rather wish to speak with full confidence upon the subject. Perhaps this sort of inquiry has been complacently avoided because it was considered dangerous by gifted men who hastened to fulfill their promise—who feared its efficacy might be lost if they questioned it too deeply. All purposes endure: we force them into life through faith or facile self-persuasion; and so, for *us*, they do live. (Consider the shepherd, whose voice is echoed mockingly by neighboring rocks; yet, in his ear, never echoed so.) Be that as it may, I still find contentment and wisdom in shedding even a fading light on the basic reasons for this vocation.

So, now, to come back to that startling question I asked a few moments ago (when I boldly expressed my doubts about the legitimate function of literature—whereas I should perhaps have been content to wreathe its altar)—to come back to that sort of indefinable attack I made (bereft though I am of the power to make it), I would reply with conscious exaggeration (and now you are forewarned): *Yes,* Literature *does* exist and, I may add, exists alone and all-exclusively. Such, at least, is the best name we can give to the achievement I speak of.

At any moment in history, a man may appear who will be fully forgetful—and always remember that he will be *consciously* forgetful—of the intellectual impedimenta of his contemporaries. Using the most elemental and elementary of means, he will try to discover (for example) the symphonic equation of the seasons of the year, the habits of a sunbeam or a cloud. He will make one or two observations analogous to the undulant heat or other inclemencies of the changing climate, which are the multiple sources of our passions. But in order to do so, he must re-create verse, carefully eliminate its excess matter, and show perfect reverence for the twenty-four letters of the alphabet. These he shall transform, through the miracle of infinity, into some special language of his own. Then, with some gesture, some ray of light, he shall give meaning to their symmetry. And so, at last, he will achieve that transfiguration and reach that supernatural height which are Poetry. This truly polished initiate of paradise will then possess—beyond all other wealth—the means to happiness: a principle for knowledge. And he will have a native land. Through his initiative, or through their own virtual power, these divine characters will become a work of art.

They are our heritage from the ancient books of magic, from our age-old wealth of mind; they provide us with a method of notation which spontaneously becomes Literature. A method— no! They are our *principle!* The turn of some special phrase or the meshes of a couplet are patterned on our understanding of them, and thus insights and relationships are born in us.

Except for study-sheets, rubrics, parchment, and such, I consider reading to be a hopeless occupation. So it is that all attempts at the manufacture of happiness have failed for lack of proper means. I know of cases in which even the most secret and careful of such means cannot, must not, satisfy us.

Something else! yes, it is as if the chance trembling of a page sought only hesitation and fluttered with impatience at the possibility of—something else. We know, of course, that we are subject to the absolute law which states that only what exists exists. Yet it would be obviously inconsistent to choose such an empty pretext as the basis for refusing all delusion, for we would then be refusing the very pleasure that we seek. The *beyond* is our means to that pleasure; I might almost say the "instrument" of our pleasure were it not repugnant to me to disassemble fiction in public (for it would be blasphemous to analyze the "mechanics" of literature and thus discover its chief cog—which is, in any case, nothingness). Yes, for me the miracle occurs when, in a dream of fiction, we seize the ideal which is absent here below, yet explosively present up above, and hurl it to some forbidden, thunderbolt height of heaven.

Why should we do this?

It is a game.

For just as we have the right to elicit emptiness from ourselves (hampered as we may be by reality too solidly, too preponderantly enthroned in us), so do we act that a sublime attraction may lovingly deliver us from that reality—and yet be filled with it and shed glittering lights upon it through empty space and in willful, solitary celebrations.

As for myself, I ask no less of literature. And now I am going to prove my point.

Nature exists; She will not be changed, although we may add cities, railroads, or other inventions to our material world.

Therefore, our eternal and only problem is to seize relationships and intervals, however few or multiple. Thus, faithful to some special vision deep within, we may extend or simplify the world at will.

To create is to conceive an object in its fleeting moment, in its absence.

To do this, we simply compare its facets and dwell lightly, negligently upon their multiplicity. We conjure up a scene of lovely, evanescent, intersecting forms. We recognize the entire and binding arabesque thus formed as it leaps dizzily in terror or plays disquieting chords; or, through a sudden digression (by no means disconcerting), we are warned of its likeness unto itself even as it hides. Then when the melodic line has given way to silence, we seem to hear such themes as are the very logic and substance of our soul. Yet whatever the agony may be in which the Monster writhes (as, through Her golden wounds, She pours the proof that She is always entire, always Herself), no vanquished throe may bend or cross the omnipresent Line which runs infinitely from point to point in Its creation of idea—creation perhaps unseen by man, mysterious, like some Harmony of perfect purity.

I am convinced that the constant grasp and realization of this ideal constitutes our obligation to Him Who once unleashed Infinity—Whose rhythm (as our fingers longingly seek it out among the keys of our verbal instrument) can be rendered by the fitting words of our daily tongue.

For in truth, what is Literature if not our mind's ambition (in the form of language) to define things; to prove to the satisfaction of our soul that a natural phenomenon corresponds to our imaginative understanding of it. And our hope, of course, is that we may ourselves be reflected in it.

I know that Music—at least in the usual sense of the word: that is, concert performances with strings, brass, wood winds, and occasionally libretti—has a similar though unexpressed ambition (She is never very confiding). And when, a moment ago, I was sketching those winding and mobile variations of the Idea which are the prerogative of the written word, some of you may have been reminded of certain orchestral phrasings in which we hear, first, a withdrawal to the shades, swirls and uneasy hesitation, and then suddenly the bursting, leaping, multiple ecstasy of Brilliance, like the approaching radiance of a sunrise. Yet this will all be useless until language, retempered and purified by the flight of song, has given it meaning.

So now we are reaching the end of our search. There can be— or rather there *must* be—an exchange following this triumphant contribution of Music: the written word must rise and Music must receive it for a brief plaintive space, else the efficacies of life will be blind to their own brilliance, hidden, and without release. I am asking for a total restoration, in perfect and neutral silence, whereby the mind may seek its own native land again: let us have quakes and slippings, unlimited and unerring trajectories, rich revery in sudden flight, delightful unfulfillment, some special lunge or synthesis. But let there be no sonorous tumult which could be resorbed in dreams.

The greatest and most magical writers have always realized this ambition.

These, then, will be the precise and reciprocal elements of Mystery in our possession (we can forget the old distinction between Music and Literature—the one purposely separated from the other in preparation for their ultimate meeting): Music will release the powers lying within that abstract center of hearing, and even of vision, which is Comprehension; while Comprehension, in all its spaciousness, will lend equal power to the printed page.

I suggest, at my own esthetic risk, the following conclusion (and if I were fortunate enough to win your silent approval of it, I should feel fully honored this evening): namely, that Music and Literature constitute the moving facet—now looming toward obscurity, now glittering unconquerably—of that single, true phenomenon which I have called Idea.

The one bends toward the other, submerges, then returns to the surface with its treasure; another dive, another fluctuation, and the entire cycle is created to perfection. For humanity in general, this will be done theatrically: they will sit unconsciously and hear a performance of their own greatness. The individual, on the other hand, will be enlightened by the book, his teacher and constant companion.

Now I can breathe more easily. I was not sure at the outset whether my subject would seem authentic or naturally acceptable, and I felt especially guilty about presenting it to you for the first time. But now that you have accepted my basic premise at least (as was obvious from your close and understanding attention to these hurrying, fateful, and seemingly impersonal thoughts which are new to me, but which may endure if there be general acquiescence), I have the sudden feeling that we are closer together; the clouds have dispersed. I should be delighted to chat with you informally, like friends whose only desire is to be together. Will you forgive me, then, if I linger over such a pleasure? My excuse must be the grave shadow that comes down from out of the nights of this city of yours (where only Thought is wakeful) and hovers in this room where revery seems so specially resonant. Now, I trust you will not feel that I have been "holding forth" in this little talk tonight, or simply adding to your regular courses by "teaching a lesson." Before I arrived, you may possibly have thought of me as a *chef d'école* (public opinion loses no time in applying that title to anyone who works alone and thus attracts a group of younger and more idealistic artists). Yet nothing could be further from the truth. But if you prefer to think of me as a recluse meditating in his favorite laboratory, like a mystagogue, or as an actor in reveries which still remain to be performed, then I would agree with you. But a sense of loyalty and even of duty must rouse us from these dreams; the more experienced must communicate their enthusiasms to the younger men. This custom is especially dear to me. For we have already agreed that there must be no interruption in the literary traditions of our countries—no disagreement between us. And since my own haunting desire is to graft those traditions to the prophetic dreams of our predecessors, I feel quite at home with you here this evening, standing before this group of famous men and gifted youths.

Now then, what better amusement can we find for the next few minutes than the comedy of errors and misunderstanding?

The worst misunderstanding, of course (but I know this isn't the case, and I merely indicate it now so as to have done with it), would be some unspoken disappointment on your part, ladies and patient listeners, because I have failed to murmur brilliant words of wisdom to a piano accompaniment or speak with authority of the books you read dreamily in your leisure hours. But then, whatever I said would be superfluous, since you all turn your writing talents to the fullest and most essential account. When I was on the train on my way here, I thought about the letters—unpublished masterpieces—which are the precious burden of postal bags and speeding locomotive. You are the chosen authors of that correspondence. And I reflected that when, with pen in hand, you turn to dreaming, eloquence, or charity, and magnetize some inward beauty in all its splendor, you need no black magic or science; you merely choose your white sheet of paper (gleaming like your smiles), you write, and there you are.

I should like to observe that the role of the poet is not entirely without its comic aspects.

In the public eye, he has become a pitiful prince banishing his own ghost from the sepulcher which should have buried him long since, and consigning it to legend and melodrama. And yet he is also the one we hold responsible for having confronted Society with an explosive and original idea.

Certain newspaper articles have been gossiping about my connection (oh, a very slight connection, really) with some scandal unleashed by a book which is apparently only the first installment of a general satire aimed at almost all the foremost minds of our time. It is not entirely unamusing to note how often such words as "idiot" and "madman" are used (and how seldom they are softened to "cretin" or "lunatic") and hurled like so many stones at a group of proud, obtrusive, feudal minds which are apparently threatening all Europe. But of course I dare not make fun of the good intentions of these scandal-mongers who are so stirred up over symptoms which do not exist; after all, we can never prevent people from making something out of nothing. The trouble in this particular instance is that science has seen fit to meddle with the problem—or else has been dragged into it. *Degeneration* is the title of the book in question (*Entartung* in the German); its author is M. Nordau. (I was determined to keep my statements on a general level and to name nobody. I think that I have just done so.) This popularizer has called our attention to a "fact": Nature (he notes) does not produce spontaneous or complete genius; instead, genius is in man generally and in no one particularly; She would appear, in practice (and in some occult and gratuitous fashion), to "compensate" for one exceptional faculty bestowed on man by destroying another. Now I submit that this is the kind of pseudo-righteous panacea and old wives' tale that needs clear critical judgment and some measure of pity. But to continue: this sickly genius (says Nordau) manages to draw strength from his weakness and grows toward fulfillment of his nature; in so doing, of course, he leaves enormous wreckage in his wake, i.e., his fellow citizens, like so many hospital cases or the "outs" on a voting list. Now M. Nordau's mistake is that he treats everything as wreckage; so you can see that the subtleties and arcana of physiology and destiny must not be entrusted to clean-living foremen or honest metal fitters, whose hands are somewhat too crude to treat them properly. A man like that goes only half way, you see; and if he had only added a little insight to his other faculties, he would have discovered this particular phase of poor Mother Nature's sacred laws and therefore not written his book at all.

A quite different brand of insult has appeared in the newspapers—in rather timid and mumbling fashion, which is strange. For, after all, why shouldn't the slightest suspicion be shouted through the streets? When the propaganda machines break down, we get a brief glimpse of parliamentary procedure and, in the process, the mob is rather pitifully confounded. I find the glimpse most interesting—but, unfortunately, it is only a glimpse, and the lesson thus taught so brief that the legislators can claim ignorance of the problem. In any case, I would challenge the addition of bullets and nails to the fray. These are only my own opinions, of course. Let me add that the idea of damning out-of-line writers who happen to be for—or against—blank verse is really quite ingenious. It little matters whether they stand in or above the battle in readiness for some special moment: in either case they are considered an insult to the newspaper columnist. Regardless of their treasure, they manage to heap disgrace (you would think they were dropping bombs) on the organization that does of course keep us posted (at great expense) on the capital's most recent apotheoses. Let's just be sure that that organization has neither first nor last say in the matter of those particular splendors which human language can find within itself. I wish we would stop insinuating and speak out loud and bold, saying that we approve the inviolability and seclusion of certain outstanding men. Whenever the masses are being herded indiscriminately toward self-interest, amusement, or convenience, it is essential that a very few disinterested persons should adopt an attitude of respectful indifference toward those common motivations and, by so doing, create a minority. And be it always understood that however broad and deep those differences may be which are created by the mad struggles of the citizenry, they must all ultimately agree that the reason for their internecine warfare is of prime importance. Now, since we can grant the need for such a minority—for this salt of the earth, this truest exception to the rule, these few chosen minds working and living here to absolute perfection—what name can best praise them? Are they laborers for love, strangers, laborers in vain? Or are they, more simply, men of letters?

I see that I have failed to brighten the rather sombre tones of our discussion; the dogmatic touch was still there, even though I tried to make fun of the man in the street with his wild attacks on anyone who is impractical enough to gather and preserve the riches of the spirit. Perhaps it was because of the disturbing atmosphere so inherent in my subject, or perhaps its dark, persistent resonance. In any case, my firework seems to have hung fire.

Which is probably just as well.

Seriously, I feel I can bring our discussion to a close now. And while I have no sense of guilt about it, I am still amazed that we had to examine poets in such an ambiguous light and subject them to twin fires of unintelligence.

It will always be the pleasure and duty of the thoughtful

critic to see through the ups and downs of a changing present
and show the truly glorious artists in perspective. But in the
meantime the disinterested poet, eschewing all virtuosity and
bravado, must project his vision of the world and use the languages of the school, home, and market place which seem most
fitting to that purpose. Then poetry will be lifted to some frightening, wavering, ecstatic pitch—like an orchestral wing spread
wide in flight, but with its talons still rooted deep within your
earth. Wherever you find it, you must deny the ineffable; for
somehow it will speak.

Thus if the common man, neighbor to us all, has the gift of
language on his lips and follows this very ordinary—or, rather,
extraordinary!—method; and if an unheard echo joins his song,
he will be able to communicate in the common vocabulary with
all pomp and light. For it is fitting that to each of us Truth be
revealed in Her native magnificence. And so, like a dutiful son
or taxpayer, he willingly contributes what he owes to the common treasure of the fatherland.

Because (I must insist upon this last point—it all stems from
that poetic Celebration we have been speaking about for the
past hour; and, rather than divide it into the elements of Music
and Literature, we can call it "Mystery" or perhaps "the evolu-
tive context of the Idea"—I must insist) *because* . . .

Throughout the centuries, *our earthly society has been seriously handicapped* because we have failed to consider brute
reality—city, government, laws—as a group of symbols. Or, to
put it another way, we have turned them into cemeteries and
thus destroyed the paradise they should be. We have made them
a terrace, hardly higher than the earth. But, despite all appear-
ances, it is not on earth, nor in tolls and elections, that we can
find the lofty drama of the formalities which create a popular
cult; for these are rather the representatives of the great Law
as It is miraculously instituted with all transparent purity.

Whenever you are in danger of losing this perspective, you
must destroy all material substructures. Or, better still, stream

fairy lights along them all—and see! Your thoughts must ask an image of your earth.

If, in days to come, a new religion rises up in France, it will be the heavenly instinct within each one of us, expanded to the dimensions of infinite joy. A relatively harmless and elementary example of this can be found on the political level: voting (even for oneself) will not be satisfying until it becomes that expansive, trumpeting hymn of joy in which no name is chosen; nor can revolutions quite provide the broil and tempest in which we must stream and sink if we would rise and be reborn as heroes.

I shall stop now, especially because I do not wish to go too far—for once, at least!—with this all-inclusive subject which is the art of letters; and also because, ineffectual as I am as a jester, Ladies and Gentlemen, I should prefer—I know that we are agreed in this—to avoid the folly that there would surely be in prophesying.

Hamlet

FAR REMOVED FROM EVERYTHING, autumnal Nature prepares Her Theater sublime and pure. She will not, in Her solitude, shed light upon essential miracles until the Poet, whose lucid eye alone can penetrate their meaning (and that meaning is the destiny of man), has been called back to ordinary cares and pleasures.

I am back again now, forgetting dead-leaf bitterness; and I should like to note down the impressions that a few of my friends and myself have had of rather banal Evenings which even the loneliest among us cannot fail to consider as he dresses for the theater. He does so in order to protract his feeling of uneasiness, well aware (because certain laws are still unfulfilled) that the extraordinary moment is no longer, or not yet, at hand.

> And now, oh child cut off from glory,
> You feel the wind in the absurd night,
> Upon your pale forehead as white as milk,
> Blowing your black feather
> And caressing you, Hamlet, oh young Hamlet!
>   (Théodore de Banville)

That adolescent who vanished from us at the beginning of his life and who will always haunt lofty, pensive minds with his mourning is very present to me now as I see him struggling against the curse of having to appear. For that is precisely, uniquely the kind of character that Hamlet externalizes on the stage, in an intimate and occult tragedy; his name, even when posted, has a fascination for me, and for you who read it, which approaches anguish. I am thankful that chance has drawn me away from my imaginative and absent-minded vision of the theater of clouds and truth, brought me down to a human stage, and given me, as my first topic of discussion, what I consider to be *the* play. For had it become too quickly disaccustomed to the purple, violet, pink, and eternally gold horizon, my vision might easily have been offended. My relationship with the skies, which were my home, now ends; and my place in front of that screen of glory is not taken by any of my indelicately palpable contemporaries. (Farewell to the brilliance of that yearly holocaust which has flamed out to the proportions of all time, so that there may be no witness to its empty rite.) And now here comes *the prince of promise unfulfillable*, young shade of all of us; and therefore there is myth in him. The lonely drama that he plays! This walker in a labyrinth of agitation and grievance so prolongs its windings with his unfinishing of an unfinished act, that he sometimes seems to be the only reason for the existence of the stage and of the golden, almost moral, space which the stage protects. For remember! Here is the only plot in drama: the struggle, in man, between his dream and the fates allotted to his life by evil fortune.

It is true that the chief interest today lies in the interpretation; but of this it was impossible to speak without having first compared it to the concept of the play.

What I shall say now has been inspired by the leading actor.

Single-handedly, through divination, through an incomparable technical mastery, and also by virtue of his literary faith in the always unfailing and mysterious beauty of the role, he was able to weave some nameless evil spell which stole into the air of this imposing performance. I have no objection to the location of the magnificent site or to the sumptuous costumes which were worn, even though, according to the latest erudite craze, they are dated (but are they really?); and even though the choice of the Renaissance period (cleverly and mistily covered up by a touch of Northern fur) is detrimental to the original perspective of the legend. One result is that the characters are made to look like contemporaries of the dramatist. Hamlet himself avoids this mistake with the traditional scantiness of his dark dress, looking a little like a Goya. This work of Shakespeare is so well patterned on the theater of the mind alone—this being the prototype of all others—that it makes no difference whether or not it is adapted for modern production. What bothers me is something other than tiny details which are infinitely difficult to regulate, in any case, and debatable at best: that is, a quality of intelligence belonging exclusively to the Parisian location of Elsinore, or—to borrow the philosophers' language—the "error of the *Théâtre-Français*." But it is the error of no one person; and in this performance the élite company was duly acclaimed for its energetic attention to detail. They certainly want to do Shakespeare, and they want to do him well. Talent, however, is not sufficient; there must be certain ingrained habits of understanding and interpretation. Here was Horatio, for example (although I am not particularly concerned with him), with something classical and Molieresque about him. Then Laertes (here I *am* concerned) played downstage and for his own sake, as if his travels and paltry twin griefs were of special interest. Even the finest of qualities must remain relatively unimportant in a story which dwells solely on an imaginary and somewhat abstract hero. Otherwise the reality of the atmosphere created by the symbolic Hamlet will be disintegrated like a curtain of mist. Actors, it must be so! For in the ideal stage performance, everything must be carried out *in obedience to a symbolic relationship of characters, either to themselves or to a single figure.* For example, an actor shows intensity and unstinting zest in a masterful rendition of Polonius, and turns him into the foolish, eager, senile steward of a merry tale. I do not entirely object to this. But in so doing he is forgetting an entirely different official whom I used to enjoy in retrospect: a figure I like to imagine as being cut out of a threadbare arras, like the one he must hide behind to die; a colorless, unsubstantial, aged clown whose almost weightless corpse, abandoned halfway through the play, has no importance save in the brusque and wild-eyed exclamation: "A rat!" Whoever hovers around an exceptional character such as Hamlet, is merely Hamlet himself. And, with his useless sword-point, the prophetic prince, destined to perish on the threshold of manhood, melancholically pushes that heap of garrulous nothingness off the path which he himself cannot follow—heap which he in turn might be, if he grew old. Ophelia, virgin child in the mind of the pitiful royal heir, was played in the modern conservatory style: she was natural, as the ingenues would have her; and rather than succumb to her songs, she preferred to use all the everyday knowledge of an experienced actress. She has a certain perfection in her tone, not without a grace of its own, which is evident in her performances and in her personality. And now, in my memory, beside the letters which spell out the name of Shakespeare, I find certain names flitting about which it would be sacrilegious even to shroud in silence, because we can divine them.

How great the power of Dreams is!

What exactly is that nameless, subtle, faded self-effacement (like the coloring of old fairy-tales) which is missing from the work of certain masters who like to make things plain, clear, and brand-new? Hamlet (a stranger everywhere) brings that quality to bear upon the hard and overly obtrusive, through the disquieting and funereal invasion of his presence. Whenever the French version of the play becomes a little too exclusively patterned, the actor restores things to their proper places; with a gesture, he exorcizes and neutralizes the pernicious influence of the *Théâtre-Français;* and, at the same time, breathes out the atmosphere of genius; all this he does with a masterful touch, because he has looked into this time-honored text with simplicity, as in a mirror. His charm lies entirely in a sort of disconsolate elegance, and lends a kind of cadence to his every start. Then there is the longing for his early and still unforgotten wisdom, despite the aberrations caused by the storm as it assails the delightful feather in his cap. Such, it would seem, is the distinctive characteristic and inventiveness in the acting of this man who, from an instinct which is sometimes obscure even to himself, draws forth the intuitions of the learned. In this way, it seems to me, he renders the morbid duality so typical of Hamlet: mad, yes, in outward appearance, whipped as he is in both directions by his duty; but oh! nonetheless, his eyes are still upon an image of himself within, and this he keeps intact—like an Ophelia still undrowned!—always prepared to get his balance back again. Jewel intact in the midst of chaos.

From the plastic and mental points of view, the tragedian, mime, and thinker is a prince of the dramatic art in his interpretation of Hamlet; and, above all, he gives us the Hamlet who has been bequeathed to contemporary minds. It was fitting, after the painful vigil of the Romantic period, that we should have at least one chance to see the essence of that magnificent daemon reach us; his bearing will not, perhaps, be understood in days to come, but the accomplishment remains. Solemnly, this actor has drawn a portrait which is immortal, lucid, somewhat composite and yet quite unified, and somehow authenticated by the seal of a supreme and timeless age; and he has given it to a future which will probably care nothing for it, but which, in any case, will be unable to alter it.

Ballets

LA CORNALBA delights me; she seems almost naked in her dance. For in an effortless rise and fall, this creature now in flight, now drowsed in veils, is summoned into the air and seems to hang there, purely Italian in the soft stretching of her body.

Is that, for lack of any other Poetry, the only memory remaining from the performance at the Eden theater? By no means! For what we call Poetry is, on the contrary, abundant there (a most pleasant interlude for a mind now free of characters in costumes and dresses, reciting immortal verse). But the magic spell of the libretto does not come out in the performance. I leaf through the program and learn that the very stars themselves— which, I am firmly convinced, should be but rarely disturbed, and even then only for high reasons of meditative gravity (in this case, according to the accompanying explanation, it is Cupid who moves and assembles them)—the very stars are present! And now the incoherent, haughty absence of meaning which twinkles in the alphabet of Night yields and, with a few starry pin-pricks in a blue curtain, spells out VIVIANE, the tempting name of the fay and title of the poem. For, of course, the *corps de ballet,* grouped in its entirety around the *star* (what name could be more suitable to her!), cannot figure the ideal dance of the constellations. No! and you can see what a plunge this meant into other worlds, straight to the depths of art! The snow, too: no dance of whiteness back and forth, no waltz can keep each flake alive; and so it is with the vernal thrust of blossoms. All that which is Poetry—nature brought to life—leaves the libretto and freezes in cardboard equipment and in the glittering stagnancy of purple and yellow muslin. Then again, as far as stage movement goes, I saw a magic circle which was certainly not drawn by the fay's own endless round or by her silken cords. Innumerable little clever details, yet none of which assumes any normal, established function in the reproduction. Going back to the "starry" example just mentioned, has there ever been a more heroic refusal of the temptation to understand not merely analogies of high seriousness, but also this law: that the chief goal of the dance, apart from its mechanics, is a mobile, unending, ubiquitous synthesis of the attitudes of each dance group, a synthesis which they must fraction ad infinitum? Hence an equal exchange resulting in the de-individualization of the coryphee, of the group, of the dancing entity, which is therefore always a symbol, never a person.

Here is a judgment, *here* is an axiom for the ballet!

I mean that the ballerina *is not a girl dancing;* that, considering the juxtaposition of those group motifs, *she is not a girl,* but rather a metaphor which symbolizes some elemental aspect of earthly form: sword, cup, flower, etc., and that *she does not dance* but rather, with miraculous lunges and abbreviations, writing with her body, she *suggests* things which the written work could *express* only in several paragraphs of dialogue or descriptive prose. Her poem is written without the writer's tools.

Following a legend came the Fable: not at all in the classical or *deus ex machina* tradition, but in a more limited sense: simply the transposition of human character and gesture to the purely animal level. This involved a rather facile re-translation of the human feelings which the fabulist had attributed to his enamored and wingèd creatures; here the characters were, indeed, more perfectly instinctive in their silent leaps than those who are given a conscious language to speak on the stage. The dance must be all wings; there must be birds, flights to the never-never land, and quivering descents like those of arrows. That, precisely and ideally, is what one should see in a performance of *The Two Pigeons:* namely, the predetermined sequence of the fundamental motifs of the Ballet. It should not be difficult for the imagination of the spectator to find such connections; but in this case it was difficult to find even a slight resemblance, and in art it is the result that counts. Delusion! except for the first act, in which we saw the love-birds turned, in an attractive incarnation, into mimicking, dancing human beings.

Two pigeons loved with a tender love,

two, or rather several pairs on a roof-top which could be seen, like the sea, through the archway of a Thessalian farm; and they were alive, not painted, which made for depth and exquisite taste. Each love-bird points to the others, then to himself, thus awakening to language through comparison. And so, little by little, the couple recalls the dove-cote with its pecking, flitting, swooning little ways; and at last the others, in delightful imitation, come invading, gliding down upon them from their frolics in the air. Now the two are children, now birds, now children once again, depending on our vision of this game of doubles and exchanges which male and female play henceforth and play forever—nothing more nor less than the game between the sexes! But now I must avoid any further consideration suggested by the Ballet—that catalyst and paradise of all spirituality—because after this simple prelude, nothing deserved even a momentary backward glance; absolutely nothing, save the perfection of the dancers. It would be tiresome to point out the foolish nothingness which followed the graceful motif of the prelude. One might mention the wanderer's flight which did, at least, conjure up that heavenly inability to disappear that keeps the ballerina's toes delightfully on the stage. And then when home calls once again, when the sweet, poignant hour of the prodigal has come (including a celebration), and when the heartrent lovers, all flight and forgiveness, reunite, there will be . . . well, you can imagine the final triumphant dance hymn, with the fiancés together again in drunken joy after the space between them, brought about by that unavoidable flight, has been gradually reduced to nothing! It will be . . . why, as if the whole thing were taking place right in your own home, ladies and gentlemen, with an appropriate kiss (quite inappropriate in art); for the Dance is only the mysterious and sacred interpreta-

tion of such a scene. But then, if we take that view, a little run
on the flute will remind us that our vision is ridiculous in the
eyes of our vulgar contemporaries, whom we must allow for,
after all, out of consideration for the theater's tickets.

There was a very clearly discerned relationship between the
usual lines of the dancer's flight and several choreographic effects; and there was the (not entirely ingenuous) fitting of the
Fable to the Ballet. Apart from these, there was simply a love
story. During the interlude of this uniquely shreds and patches
performance, the wondrous and matchless virtuosa Mlle. Mauri
summed it up, mingling her divination with pure and trembling
animality. At every point she indicated the allusions which had
not yet been brought into perfect focus; and with a touch of
her fingers, just before she took a step, she would call a shimmering fold forth from her skirt and seem to fly up to the Idea
on impatient wings.

The historical scenic art form is the Drama. The Ballet, on
the contrary, is a symbolic form. The two should be allied, but
not confused. You must not give brusque and common treatment to two attitudes which are jealous of their respective gifts
of silence. Acting and dancing become suddenly hostile whenever they are forcibly brought together. For example: when the
attempt was made just now to show forth the single essence of a
bird through twin performers, it was decided (you will remember) to pair a mime and a ballerina. But they are too unlike!
If one is a dove, why, the other will be . . . Lord knows! perhaps the breeze. Fortunately, at the Eden theater, the exclusive
qualities of the two art forms were most judiciously observed:
the hero living in his twin worlds—a child still, and yet a man—
was set in thematic opposition to the rival heroine who was both
a woman *walking* toward him on royal carpets and also the original fay, equally important with her flutterings. This distinction of each scenic genre, in contact or opposition with the
other, becomes the controlling feature of the work, and the
resulting disparity is used for its very structure. But a communication between the two still remains to be found. Ordinarily,

the librettist fails to understand that the ballerina expresses herself with steps, and that beyond this she has no eloquence, not even that of gesture.

Even if genius should say: "The Dance is a figuration of caprice in rhythmical flight. Here, with their numbers, are the few basic equations of all fantasy; and the human form in its most excessive mobility, in its truest development, cannot escape them, insofar, of course, as they are a visual embodiment of the idea"—and now take a glance at any choreographic ensemble, and compare!—there is still no one who would accept this method of setting up a ballet. The modern cast of mind is well known and, even in the case of those whose faculties are exceptional when used, it must be replaced by some nameless, impersonal, glittering glance of absoluteness, like that lightning which has in recent years enveloped the ballerinas at the Eden theater, fused its naked electricity with paints of a whiteness beyond the ken of flesh, and surely made of her that wondrous being who has drawn back beyond all conceivable living worlds.

At those times when we ordinarily watch the Dance with no special object in mind, the only way to lead our imagination on is to stand patiently, calmly watching each of the dancer's steps, each strange pose—toeing, tapping, lunge, or rebound—and then ask ourselves: "What can the meaning of it be?" Or, better still, find inspiration suddenly and interpret it. Doubtless that will mean living entirely in the world of revery. World sufficient, nonetheless; nebulous or clear, spacious or limited—any of these, so long as that illiterate ballerina, flutteringly engaged in her profession, encloses it with her circlings or bears it off in flight.

Oh, stranger to me and yet a Friend, as you sit hidden some evening in the theater: if, at that sorceress' feet (she! all unaware of sorcery), you will but humbly place the Flower *of your poetic instinct* (like those roses which are thrown off and up into visible higher worlds by a flick of her pale and dizzying satin slippers), drawing from this alone the true light and revelation of your numberless secret imaginings, then (in an exchange which seems to be the secret and revelation of her smile), through her always ultimate veil, she will give you back your concepts in all their nakedness, and silently inscribe your vision as would a Symbol —which she is.

Solemnity

PROUDLY INCOMPETENT AS I AM in all matters not pertaining to the Absolute, I cannot decide which of the following is the more abominable: the salesman-like intruder whose artistic merchandise differs somewhat in nature from ecstasy and celebration; or the ineffectual priest, with his ineffectual trappings, conducting a service all unabashed.

It is bad enough to stuff the theater with insolent gimmicks and dummies and to exclude the sublime manifestations of Poetry which the spectator always hopes to see. It is even worse to exhibit Poetry in ways which are especially conducive to a yawn; if the Deity has to be strapped in some hulking, vulgar apparatus, it would be just as well perhaps to omit Him altogether.

My objection to false temples—even if their name should be *Odéon*—is not that they adopt one method or another (for the method will always be adaptable to their pseudo-nature and will depend on their architecture); but rather that theirs is the facade of a false cult in which a vestal virgin is kept around to feed the pharmaceutical tripod-flame of "real, honest-to-goodness art!" and that they rush meticulously and unsuspectingly to a patent medicine which has some such negligible name as *Ponsard* on the label—as if they were rushing to find something essential and true! It is unjust to the immediate past and future to say (and the claim unfortunately seems to have received the stamp of national approval) that the present day is lacking in such products, from the points of view of quantity and quality; it is like filling the emptiness of the nonexistent with the nonexistent. On the contrary, according to my *Notes* especially, we are in the worst possible state. Oh, cold-crypt priestess! you shouldn't have taken down one of those clever flasks which economize by covering themselves from birth with the dust of eternity. If Ponsard galls me particularly, it is because of the way he made his reputation: with a fantastic, foolhardy, extravagant, almost splendid effrontery—and with a total absence of brilliance in the performance—he persuaded a clique that he was bringing Poetry to the stage; and all the while the god of Poetry still shone brightly forth. I admire the way he noticed Hugo and took the hint: low-born, weak, and without talent, he pretended to be obliged to rise to giddy heights of art because no one else was available; and, when all is said and done, he struggled hard and achieved a vigorousness quite worthy of papier-mâché. A most clever and amusing operation, one which many of us will remember. However, there is no immediate need to call in the new generation to commemorate it. But how fond I am, in the secrecy of my simple, honorable heart, of the authentic substitutes of the Poet (although I would not have them revived to the detriment of any of my contemporaries)! They suffer our smile—or their own, perhaps, if they put one on; for their desire, in all modesty, is to abolish the existence of that disastrous, empty span of time caused by the total extinction of lyricism, by the Luce de Lancivals, the Campistrons, and other shades. They have covered what used to be their soul with an old artistic rag, threadbare even in its technique; they refuse to admit that the Goddess' veil has been snatched off and ripped from end to end; She is in mourning. These specters will always touch us deeply; I feel sorry, too, for their offspring: they can be compared to people protecting altars with fists closed tight in desperation—and also in boredom. Not only are all these imitators and precursors grotesque, but they can even teach us a lesson: as a sort of sacred trust, they receive from one century (and hand on to the next) something which does not exist (or if it does, it would be better not to know anything about it!): namely, a residue of art, axioms, formulae, nothing.

One evening when all magnificence and joy were gone, I sought compensation in that radiant work *Le Forgeron,* that I might learn some lonely truths.

Anything composed in disobedience to the venerable genius of verse is not a poem. Rhyme in this work is extraordinary because it is an integral part of the alexandrine; and the alexandrine with its multiple attitudes and gestures seems to be entirely swallowed up by it, vanquished even in its first syllable by that glittering source of ecstasy. Before rhyme assumed this function, before it began its sudden fluttering and rise from earth, the attempt was—and the attempt each day now is—to possess and establish the notion of a certain concept. But it is undeniable that the notion—in the usual definition of the word —must now be forgotten, and we must henceforth work only with the dialectic of Verse. For Verse is jealous rival and master to the yielding dreamer. Without It, all discourse (however beautiful, however self-assured, however philosophical, however imaginative or brilliant, however celestial a vision of humanity it may be—like Banville's work)—without It, all discourse would be simply spoken words. But Verse revives it all and lifts it all to heights of glory. Through a sublime metamorphosis, all conditions and materials of thought are uprooted from their natural prose site and entirely transformed. After that change, after that flight to heaven, words reach their efficacy.

It is clear that ever since the phenomenon Poetry first astonished the earth, no one perhaps has practiced it with the bold candor exhibited by the instant and elemental mind of Théodore de Banville. The ever-increasing purification of his poetic personality has now made of him an exceptional, superior individual; he drinks in loneliness at a hidden and eternal spring. He has returned to youth in that admirable direction the child takes in order to be nearer to purity and nothingness. And so it is not mere enthusiasm or the delirium common to lyric poets that lifts him endlessly to his heights; but rather, all undistilled inspiration is put away, and words in all their efficacy are fitted out and joined in a unique and perfect prosody, which asks of the hidden poet (who is Every Reader) that he should sing the song according to the modulations of the sweet or brilliant.

Thus, all unaided, that principle springs up which is simply Verse! And as it blooms, in and out it breathes those countless elements of beauty hastening to gather there in the order of their elemental value, to glitter there a moment, and to die in an ephemeral flowering—within a world translucent, like some ethereal world. Symbol! living in the abyss and center of that spiritual world wherein it is impossible that anything should be the exclusive property of the Whole; Symbol, the heavenly numerator of our apotheosis; Symbol, the supreme and nameless mold which bears no palpable existence within itself, but gathers all scattered, unsuspected, richly hovering treasures, forges them, and brands them with its seal.

That is why (as I should now observe) verses in our language go only in pairs or still greater numbers, because of their final harmony. This is the mysterious law of Rhyme, the guardian angel who appears in order that no single verse may be usurper or stand decisively alone. With what end in view a given verse is made, I care not: it is not a question of its composition and gratuitous aspect; it must rather hang in a momentary, twin balance (as if it were in flight), in an identity of two constituent elements which are reproduced externally in their consonant equality.

Such are the saintly laws of this the first and last of all the Arts; and every page of every book announces them, shoots them high to heaven like arrows of shimmering gold. Such is the intellectual spectacle which fascinates me. Comparable to it is another, which stems from fable or fiction.

Venus, born of Love, is immediately coveted by Jupiter and the Olympians. To reduce the havoc this virgin can cause (and since she must not be common property), they command her to enter into wedlock with Vulcan, the promising artisan of master-works. These the virgin, who is all human Beauty, will syn-thesize; and thus, by her choice, she will repay him (one has to give the plot of this work to begin with, in a minimum of words, because words are its very substance).

What a performance! It contains the world. Whenever the book we read proposes a lofty idea, it supplants all theaters, not by making us forget them, but, on the contrary, by recalling them with sovereign power. That metaphorical sky which mush-rooms out in the vicinity of the poem's lightning is the perfect artifice; in this way, little by little, heroes are feigned and then embodied (with just the proper touch to make them visible yet unobtrusive). That spiritually, magnificently illuminated sky of ecstasy is the very purity which we carry in ourselves eternally —purity prepared to burst forth at those moments which do not occur in real life, i.e., outside of art. This is music which or-chestral instruments tend simply to reproduce, to simulate. How admirable the omnipotent simplicity of this elocution, this faith in the common and superior language! How admirable, too, the prosody which polishes such elocution for its ultimate expres-sion. So that Banville's mind, taking refuge within these several pages, defies civilization, which neglected to construct the mi-raculous Theater and Stage which the mind envisions, to which the mind alone can give true existence. The actor is absent; absent, too, the woodwinds, brasses, and strings with their prel-udes and finales; and the mind, living beyond all materiality, accepts or refuses at will the accompaniment of the arts. He has come alone at the appointed hour (the appointed hour is any hour, as well as never), and, like a messenger, he brings the book to us with gesture or with voice, then disappears. Thus, he who held a dazzling light generally multiplies it in us all, communi-cates.

The miracle of great poetry such as this would seem to me to be the following: whenever conditions arise which permit its visible development and interpretation, it surrenders to them; and with a sort of adaptable ingenuousness it can replace all things, simply because all things are absent. I should imagine that when, in the future, we come together for the celebrations which are listed upon the human program, the cause for doing so will not be the theater, limited as it is and by itself unable to respond to the subtlest of human instincts; nor music, which is in any case an art too fleeting to interest the mob sufficiently; but rather it will be the Ode, assimilating such over-misty, over-palpable elements as the theater and music tend to isolate; It will be dramatized and knowingly divided; heroic scenes will be simply an ode for many voices.

Yes, truly! think, think what that cult could be, which is destined for such celebration! Simply the ancient, the eternal cult which was almost drowned in darkness by the recent tide of the symphony concert, whereas it should have been set free to reign upon the very stage where it had been improperly enthroned.

Even in the case of Wagner (the most haughtily French of poets begs his forgiveness for failing to discuss him here at length), I would not, in the strictest sense of the word, speak of theater (without any doubt, there is much more of the dramatic in Greece or in Shakespeare). His is rather a vision of legend which lives for itself beneath a veil of sounds, and mingles with them. His scores, moreover, compared to those of a Beethoven or a Bach, are not merely musical. Something more special, something more complex is involved: namely, Fiction or Poetry, which lies at the crossroads of the other arts, stems from them, and yet controls them.

The kind of work that Théodore de Banville has given us, in the maturity of his wisdom and power, is essentially literary; yet it is not entirely adapted to the technique of that spiritual instrument par excellence, which is the Book. The actor should steal into the display of poetic attitudes, fit his words to them, and enter into the silences of the orchestra; symphonic richness should translate the scattered lines of prose as they move forth decked out in precious stones and veils (which are best displayed when never seen); each scene should be a perfectly ideal setting or site to deify the actor as he approaches, summoned, as he is, merely to appear now through the very breach which the amplitude and majesty of that site have made. I state without reservation that if those conditions were observed, this most magnificent of spectacles would be, in our esthetic or industrial age, the logical climax and conclusion of the entire artistic surge which was necessarily limited to matters of technical invention during the Renaissance period. Splendid, grandiose, impelling development! This recitation (a term which we must always come back to when poetry is under discussion) will fascinate, instruct, and above all it will astound the People, despite its classical origin—classical in the sense that the gods will have flown up and back to their ideal form; and, after all, there has been no progress in mythical invention. In any case, no other way we know of can so perfectly furnish the sort of text which offers delight and official ceremonies in a taste at once ancient and modern. And so we shall have the Opening of a Jubilee; especially of that figurative jubilee which must conclude a cycle in History and, to this end, must have, I think, the ministry of the Poet.

Richard Wagner, Revery of a French Poet

A CONTEMPORARY FRENCH POET who, for several reasons, takes no part in official displays of beauty would like now to continue along the lines of his daily task (which is the mysterious polishing of verse for lonely Celebrations) and meditate upon the majestic ceremonies of Poetry. These are incompatible with the flood of banality borne along by the arts of our sham civilization. They are the ceremonies of a day which lies unborn within the unsuspecting womb of the people. They are almost a Cult!

Certainly neither this poet nor his contemporaries will be involved in any such ceremony, and therefore his dream need not be troubled by any sense of incapability or by its own distance from reality.

His clear and peaceful vision extends afar.

The least he can do, then—accepting the challenge—is to look only upon the Chimaera-Who-cannot-Be, braving the proud coils of Her consequences; then, pierce Her side with a pure and affirmative glance.

For the moment, this worshipper of poetry will pass over the extraordinary, but as yet unperfected, display of the plastic arts (the Dance being chief among them, at least in the perfection of its expression; and, by virtue of the conciseness of its writing, only the Dance can translate the fleeting and the sudden into the Idea. To see this is to see the entire—absolutely the entire—Spectacle of the future).

Now, if he considers Music's rightful contribution to the theater—a quickening and conjuring of Its spirit—he does not hesitate for long. For whatever the leaps and directions of his thought may be, he feels the colossal approach of an Initiation. Oh poet, see if your desire is not now fulfilled!

Oh strange defiance hurled at poets by him who has usurped their duty with the most open and splendid audacity: Richard Wagner!

There have been varying reactions to this foreigner: ecstasy, worship, yet also an uneasy feeling because his compositions do not appear to radiate directly, in their execution, from literary principle.

It is difficult to judge him fairly. In order to do so, we must understand the situation in which this Master first found himself. He comes along at a time—the only time—when our theater can rightly be called "decadent," so crude are the elements which compose its Fiction. For it simply looms up suddenly and asks us to believe in the reality of its characters and plot—simply to *believe,* and that is all. But this belief demanded of the spectator should, on the contrary, consist of the total strength which he elicits from the combination of all the arts; and the theatrical miracle which these arts perform will be motionless and insubstantial in an entirely new sense. We must undergo a spell. And if that spell is to be woven, we must accept every available means of enchantment which the magic of music offers, so that our reason may be defeated when it is at grips with a symbol. But then our theater comes along and exclaims: "Just imagine that this is really happening and that you are there!"

The theater-goer of today scorns imagination; but he is skilled in making use of the arts, and he wants each of them to transport him to a place where a special power of illusion will be released. If so, he will go along.

And yet the pre-Musical Theater was of necessity based on that authoritarian and simple-minded idea, because its masterpieces could not benefit from this new means of evocation; because, alas! they lay quietly in the sacred pages of the book and could not hope to spring up from them and join our ceremonies. This Theater belongs strictly to the past; and because of its intellectual despotism, it would, in any case, be overthrown by a performance for the people, who wish only to receive *suggestion* from art, so that they may be masters of their own belief. Now that Music has been added, everything is completely changed. The central principle of the old Theater has been annihilated. Now stage performance has become strictly allegorical, empty, abstract, impersonal; now, in order to rise up and resemble truth, it must be revived in the life-giving breath poured out by Music.

Music's mere presence will constitute a triumph, provided that it is not brought to bear upon the outmoded methods of the Theater (even though it might be able to expand them to perfection). Music must burst forth and regenerate all vitality. Then the audience will feel that if the orchestra suddenly stopped pouring forth its influence, the actor would immediately become a statue.

How, then, could this Musician reduce the function of Art to this primary aim and, at the same time, remain the close confidant of his own Art's secret? To accomplish that metamorphosis, he had to possess the disinterestedness of a critic, and forget that behind him, wildly and joyfully prepared to rush forth, lay the most tumultuous abyss of musical execution that any man has ever mastered with his lucid will.

This is what he did.

Proceeding immediately to the essentials, he combined an entire tradition, still intact but almost obsolete, with the fresh and hidden springs which he could divine in its music. Refusing analysis (which would have meant a fruitless suicide), this creator so used the singular, rich gift for synthesis which lived within him, that he was able to marry two elements of beauty which are mutually exclusive or at least unrelated: intimate drama and ideal music. Yes! Through this harmonious compromise, he restored a particular aspect of the theater which miraculously corresponds to the musical disposition of his race.

Even though, logically speaking, Music is thereby simply added to Drama, nevertheless it penetrates, envelops, and joins it by virtue of the composer's dazzling will. (Oh, who can tell the origin of Music, its first meaning and its fates?) There is no simplicity, no depth, which Music, once it is aroused, cannot lavish on this pattern. But in its principle, it escapes us.

A miraculous delicacy is required if these dissimilar forms of pleasure, scenic and orchestral, are to be merged without either one of them being totally transformed.

Now at last we have music which is obedient only to its own most complex laws, above all to the vague and the intuitive. First it mingles the colors and forms of the actor with its own timbres and motifs, thereby creating a richer atmosphere of Revery than would be possible for any earthbound melody; creating a deity draped in the invisible folds of a musical texture. And then it sweeps him away in a wave of Passion which is too furiously unleashed to be borne by one alone; hurls him down, twists him about, and even robs him of his senses (they are lost in this superhuman rush), only to give them back again, so that he may be all-victorious in a song which bursts through the agony of creative thought. The hero, living as much in the clouds as on the earth, always appears in a distance which is filled with the mist of lamentations, victories, and joy breathed forth by the instruments. Thus he goes back to the world's beginnings. As in the Greek drama, his actions are always surrounded by the amazement and intimacy which the audience feels when it is face to face with myths. These are almost nonexistent, so fleeting is their primitive past; and yet they continue to profit from the familiar appearance of the individual actor. Indeed, certain of them satisfy us mentally because they do not seem to be entirely devoid of relationship with occasional symbols.

Here, then, on the stage, Legend is enthroned.

For the second time in history, the people (first Greek and now German) can borrow sacred feelings from the past and look upon the secret of their origins, even as that secret is being acted out. Some strange, new, primitive happiness keeps them seated there before that mobile veil of orchestral delicacy, before that magnificence which adorns their genesis.

Thus, all things are restrengthened in the primitive stream. Yet not in its spring.

It is not in this way that the strictly imaginative, abstract, and therefore poetic French mind shines forth. For that mind shrinks back from Legend; therein it resembles perfect Art, which is invention. From days gone by, the French preserve no looming, no half-misty memory; it is as if they knew in advance that to do so would be anachronistic in a theatrical performance, that is, in the Rite of one of Civilization's accomplishments. But perhaps they would accept the Fable, which lives virginally apart from all known places, times, and persons; unveiled as it rises from the unanimity of the assembled people; written on the pages of the Skies (History is merely one interpretation of it); empty; in short, a Poem or Ode. What! Has this era, has our country which spreads this era's fame, disintegrated Myths by means of thought and then gone on to make new ones! The Theater calls not for several established, eternal, or well-known Myths, but for one Myth free of individuality, since it must embrace the many aspects of human life. Art, with a magic befitting the national spirit, must evoke these aspects and mirror them in all of us. The hero must have no name, for there must be a surprise. His gesture will contain, within itself, our dreams of privileged places and of paradise—dreams which were engulfed by the old-time drama, with its foolish desire to contain them or represent them on the stage. It is he that exists, not any particular stage! (Remember the mistake the theater made, when Music was absent, with its permanent sets and real actors.) Does a gesture of our soul, do symbols in preparation or in blossom need any place for their development, other than the fictitious stage of vision which flashes in the glance of the audience? Myth is the Saint of Saints, but It must live in our imaginations. In a miraculous, supreme flash of lightning giving birth to that Figure which is No One, It embraces each acting pose fitted by the Figure to the symphonic rhythm. And thus It is set free! Then the rarefaction and heights which Music gives us seem to expire at the feet of the hero thus incarnate; and in this way they are somehow bound to his humanity, and they become the hidden, vibrant extension of all things, of Life itself.

Thus Man and his authentic paradise on earth exchange their vows.

There lies Mystery.

Thus the City, which gave us the theater for this holy experience, places on our earth the seal of the universe.

As for the City's people, the least they can do is witness the sacred act (let Justice be my witness, Justice which *must* reign there!), since that orchestra, which just now demonstrated the god's existence, distills the very same immortal, inborn subtleties and splendors which live unsuspected in the midst of a silent audience.

Oh Genius! that is why I, a humble slave to eternal logic, oh Wagner!—that is why I suffer and reproach myself, in moments

branded with weariness, because I am not among those who
leave the universal pain and find lasting salvation by going directly to the house of your Art, which is their journey's end.
In times of gladness—gladness for no single nation—this uncon-
querable portico offers us protection against our insufficiency
and the mediocrity of nations; it lifts the ardent to the heights
of certainty. For them, it is not merely the greatest journey ever
conducted under the aegis of man and your leadership: it is the
end of man's journey to an Ideal. May I at least have my share in
this delight? And half-way up the saintly mountain may I take
my rest in your Temple, Whose dome trumpets abroad the most
extensive dawning of truths ever known and, as far as the eye
can reach from the parvis, urges on the steps of your elected as
they walk upon the lawns? Thus will our minds be kept in isolation from the incoherence which pursues them; and this will
be our shelter against that threatening peak of the Absolute
which haunts us all too lucidly, while we divine its presence in
the parting of those clouds on high—glittering, naked, lonely
peak, beyond us, doubtless never to be reached by man. Never to
be reached! But the passer-by, at this thought, feels no remorse
as he drinks at your welcoming fountain.

Verlaine

THE TOMB MUST HAVE immediate silence.

Acclamation, renown, and resounding words withdraw; and
the sobbing of the songs he has abandoned must not follow him
to his hiding place. For his presence would obscure his glory.

Nor must we, on our side, several brothers in our grief, make
any literary intrusion. All the newspapers are talking about it;
it is as if the white pages of his unfinished work had grown in

size and flown off bearing news of his disappearance to the mist and to the people.

And now Death knowingly sets this tombstone here, so that henceforth we may stand upon it firmly, explain this man, and put an end to misunderstanding. We hold out our hands to the dear departed in a gesture of farewell. Can the noble human being that he was reappear, for the last time, aware that he was misunderstood, and say: "See what I really was"?

Gentlemen, let us teach the passer-by and indeed all those absent today who, through incompetence and faulty vision, may have misconstrued the outward appearance of our friend, that his bearing was, in reality, the most correct of all.

Yes, whenever youthful lips are opened for a brief hour, his poetry, from generation to generation, will pour forth a stream of song to quench their thirst in waters sweet, eternal, and purely French. Surely his nobility lies in this. But even if it were not so, we would still be called upon to weep for him and deeply worship him. We were spectators of this drama. And yet even our sympathy is powerless to alter in any way the absoluteness of the attitude that this exceptional human being assumed against Fate.

The genius of Paul Verlaine has fled to future time, and he remains a hero.

Oh, let us remember, whenever we are tempted to make some ostentatious or profitable compromise with outward reality, that he was alone; let us remember this rare occurrence in the course of centuries, that our contemporary was alone when he confronted the situation of the poet and the dreamer in all its horror. Loneliness, cold, drabness, and poverty are wounds which he could easily have answered with others self-inflicted. But, in his case, poetry was the almost sufficient answer. Such are the usual ingredients of the fate that such a child brings upon himself as he walks through life with ingenuous boldness, guided by his genius. "So be it!" answered this noble spirit. "These insults must be borne; I shall bear them to the limit, in grief and in shame."

There was scandal. Against whom? Everybody. But it was sounded abroad, accepted, and sought out by one man. He did not hide from destiny. On the contrary, he rather defiantly pressed it when it hesitated; and therefore his boldness came to be a frightening integrity. That is what we saw, gentlemen, and we are witnesses to it: witnesses to that righteous revolt wherein man appears before his Mother, whoever She may be and however disguised—as the mob, inspiration, life, or the nakedness She has clothed the poet in. And that sanctifies a fierce, loyal, and childlike heart all steeped in honor.

With this homage, Verlaine, we shall worthily say farewell to your remains.

LETTERS: *ideas on poetry*

To Henri Cazalis, June 4, 1862

Emmanuel [des Essarts] may have spoken to you about the strange feeling of sterility I have had this spring. After three futile months, I have finally gotten rid of it, and my first sonnet is meant to describe it—that is, to curse it. This kind of poem is fairly new: the physical effects of the blood and nerves are analyzed and combined with their influence on the mind and soul. It could be called: *Springtime Spleen.* If the combination is well harmonized, and if a work of that sort is neither too physical nor too spiritual, it can be rather effective.

To Henri Cazalis, June 3, 1863

I think Emmanuel is doing himself a great injustice by indulging in such facility. It is just too easy to get out those "brilliant" empty articles.

He doesn't make the proper distinction between the Ideal and the Real. Some idiotic modern poet says he is sorry that "Action isn't the sister of Dreams." Emmanuel feels the same way. Good Lord, if that were the case, if Dreams *were* withered

81

and debased, what escape would there be for those of us who are sick of the earth? Dreams are our only refuge. Oh, Henri, steep yourself in Ideal! Happiness on earth is wretched. One has to be pretty vulgar to stoop to it. To say "I am happy" amounts to saying: "I am a coward," or more often: "I am a fool."

To Henri Cazalis, April 25, 1864

Your sentences are a little too short, I think, and their harmony a little short-winded. But when I say that, I am thinking of the artist in you, not of the dreamer; for as a dreamer, you are unsurpassable. To fools, Gautier's sentences seem "plastic"; but to me, they are a miracle of balance; they have a rightness of touch which is righteousness itself; they are the perfect model of a soul who lives in Beauty. If you can just find a beauty less serene and yet a beauty which explores the deepest abyss and the seventh heaven of mysticism (*as Balzac did in Séraphita*), then your dream will achieve an even greater immateriality in the eyes of the true artist.

Great art consists of showing, through faultless self-possession, that we are on the heights of ecstasy, without revealing how we reached them.

Now, your sentences lift their arms toward the Ideal, they reach forth, and sometimes they seem to fly away. But you should make them soar.

I wonder if I can make you understand just what I mean. What I am trying to say is so intimate, so veiled, so vague, that I am afraid I have been too precise in places. Forgive me. And let me close with a recipe of my own invention; I follow it myself: "Always omit the beginning and the end of what you write. No introduction, no finale." You think I am mad? I'll show you some day that my madness lies elsewhere.

To Henri Cazalis, October, 1864

I'm hard at work. I've finally begun my *Hérodiade*—in fear and trembling, because I am inventing a new language which must arise from a completely new poetics and which I can define briefly as follows: *Describe not the object itself, but the effect it produces.* Therefore, a verse must not be composed of words, but of intentions; all words must yield to sensation. I don't know whether you see what I am getting at, but I trust you will approve me when I have succeeded. Because, for the first time in my life, *I will succeed.* If I am defeated, I shall never write again.

To Henri Cazalis, December, 1864

One of these days I will send you a new prose-poem that I don't have the strength or the time to copy now. . . . I think that as far as poetry goes, I'm done: there are vast empty spaces in my mind; I am incapable of any consistent, close thought. And so, with this all too real, all too cruel degradation of my mind (as you alone are aware, my dear fellow), I am atoning for the excesses of my youth. I look upon myself with fear, as on a ruin. In all my letters I am going to lie to my friends and tell them I am working; but it won't be true. A poet on this earth should be purely a poet; whereas I, too often, am a corpse. I may some day deserve to be considered as an amateur, but no more than that.

To Henri Cazalis, January, 1865

I am sad. A black, freezing wind won't let me walk, and I don't know what to do in the house when my wretched mind won't let me work.

And I am disgusted with myself: I draw back trembling from the mirror when I see my face so worn and gone; I weep at my emptiness and I cannot write a single word on my mercilessly white paper.

Think of my being an old man, done in, at the age of twenty-three, while my friends live in the light and among the flowers in the years when we should be writing our masterpieces. And to think that I have not even had the benefit of death, which might have convinced you all that I was worth something and that Destiny alone was to be blamed for my failure to survive.

But everything has contributed to my defeat. Weak-minded as I am, I needed all kinds of stimulation: friends with their inspiring voices, paintings, music, sound, life. The one thing on earth that I should have avoided was that solitude which quickens only the strong. But I am condemned to unparalleled solitude in an ugly land, deprived even of the presence of Nature.

A great genius, an austere thinker, or a scholar would benefit from such solitude. But the poor poet—one who is a poet only; that is, an instrument played upon by the fingers of various sensations—is silent when he lives where nothing moves him. The strings stretch, then, and dust and forgetfulness succeed.

To Eugène Lefébure, February, 1865

What I object to in Taine is his claim that an artist can be defined simply as man at his most powerful. For I believe that it is perfectly possible to have a human temperament quite distinct from the literary. That is why my attitude toward Taine is contrary to yours. I feel that for him impression is the only mainspring of works of art; he tends to lose sight of the reflective power. When the artist sits down to write, he *makes himself.* Taine doesn't believe, for example, that a writer can change his manner completely. As a matter of fact, he *can;* I have seen this in my own case. As a schoolboy, I used to write twenty-page papers and I was well known for my inability to stop. And yet, since those days, I have gone to the other extreme and tended to exaggerate my love of the concise. I used to be violently pro-lix, wildly diffuse; naturally, I wrote whatever first entered my head; I believed in stylistic effusion. What could be more dif-ferent from that sincere, impulsive schoolboy than the man of letters I now am?

Now for a small complaint: your poems are too full of "Love"; the word lacks color; it often turns up in a rather insipid fash-ion. If this vague emotion is not particularized, seasoned in some strange way by lewdness, ecstasy, sickness, or asceticism, then I don't think it is poetic. *I* could *never* write the word in a poem without smiling. Is that because it is an old expression? No, I think it is because love, being elemental, is too natural a feeling ever to arouse the blasé poets who read poetry. Speaking to *them* of love would be like offering clear, deep spring water to the inflammable, flaming, brandied palates of decrepit drunkards.

But what particularly irritates me about the word (which I can't say or write without a certain displeasure), is the silly group of fools (including E . . .) who have become self-appointed priests for the fat, red-faced, chubby butcher's boy they call Eros, and who look at each other in martyr-like ecstasy whenever they perform His facile rites and climb on the women they have seduced as they would on a funeral pyre! Who say, in short, that Love is all, when in truth it is but one of a thousand feelings that lay siege to our soul and must be given no more consideration than fear, remorse, boredom, hate, or sadness.

To Henri Cazalis, June, 1865

I will simply send you a kiss. May my lips be woman's!

And yet, they must not be, for they would bleed! They have been wounded by the flute that I have been madly playing. Yes, I began my work ten days ago.

I have left *Hérodiade* to cruel winter. I was sterilized by that lonely work. In the meantime, I am writing a heroic interlude with a Faun as the hero.

This poem is most lofty and beautiful in its conception, but the verses are tremendously difficult because I am writing it as pure theater; it will not be *playable on the stage,* but it *needs the stage.*

Yet, at the same time, I want to preserve the full poetry of my lyric verse, my own poetic instinct, and fit it to the drama. I think you'll like it when you get here. The mere thought of the last scene makes me weep. The central idea is vast, the poetry most refined.

To Henri Cazalis, July, 1865

If only I can reach a fitting conclusion to the story of my Faun! You can't imagine how difficult it is to struggle with this poetry. I want it to be very new and very beautiful, and yet dramatic; above all, it has to be more rhythmical than lyric verse, to delight the ear of the theater-goer. You can't imagine how difficult and sometimes impossible it is to keep thinking lucidly in this southern heat that alternately burns and stifles and always defeats the body. Then too, there is the maddening business of classes. They destroy my day and give me headaches. The students have very little respect for me, and occasionally I am greeted with hoots and spitballs. But if I can get enough will power and pots of coffee, I shall win out.

What you say about your aunt's and sister's reactions saddens me but doesn't surprise me, for I am utterly convinced that art is for artists alone. If you only knew how it grieves me to have to dilute and weaken my thought so that it will be immediately intelligible to an indifferent audience.

If you only knew how many nights of despair and days of dreaming I have to live, in order to write original poetry— which is something I have never done before; great, mysterious poetry which will make the poet's soul rejoice. What a deep study of sound and color, of music and painting, our thought must make (however beautiful it may have been originally) if it is to be poetic!

To Henri Cazalis, (?) *1865*

As far as I am concerned, the only thing a self-respecting man can do is to keep looking up at the sky as he dies of hunger.

To Henri Cazalis, December 5, *1865*

Forgive me for the past and the future.

For the past: because I haven't written to thank you for your splendid book. I spent the whole week suffering horribly from neuralgia. It beat at my temples day and night and wrung the nerves in my teeth. Whenever there was a let-up, I rushed madly, desperately to my table to try and write an overture for my poem. I *could* not. It eludes me. I hear it singing in me, but I cannot write it down.

For the future: because I must find isolation in the unknown regions of Revery for the sake of this enslaving work; I must have no distractions, no friendly, easy conversation. I live in inviolate solitude and silence. So this letter will have to be just a note.

Oh, I *shall* extract this poem—this magnificent jewel—from the sanctuary of my thought! Else I shall die upon the ruins. I spend every night—the only time I have to myself—dreaming about *every word*.

To Théodore Aubanel, January, *1866*

For me, the most serious thing was the recent trip which suddenly tore me away from my Dream. After that I couldn't settle down to work again. Last night I had the good fortune to see my poem again in all its nakedness. Tonight I want to try to compose it. It is so hard for me to get away from life completely enough to have an effortless feeling for those otherworldly and naturally harmonious impressions which I want to communicate; I have to concentrate with a self-restraint which borders on madness.

To Henri Cazalis, March, 1866

I must tell you about the last three months. I can't give you any details, but they were frightful. I spent them in a struggle with *Hérodiade*, as my lamp will witness! I wrote the musical overture, still just a rough draft for the most part, but I can say without any exaggeration that it is going to be magnificent. The dramatic scene I showed you is nothing: it would be like comparing a vulgar Epinal picture to a Leonardo da Vinci painting. I'm still going to need three or four winters to finish, but when it is all over, I will have what I have always dreamed of: a poem worthy of Poe, and just as good as his.

You can see how truly splendid the glimpses I have had must be if I can conquer my eternal pessimism and speak with such assurance.

But my misfortune is that, when I had polished my poetry down to this depth, I came upon twin abysses which drove me mad. The first was Nothingness, which I found without any prior knowledge of Buddhism, and I am still too heartsick to bring myself to believe in my own poetry, even; to get back to the work that I had to abandon in the face of this overwhelming vision.

Yes, yes, I *know:* we are all only empty forms of matter— empty and yet sublime, because we have invented God and our own souls. So sublime, indeed, my dear fellow, that my ambition is to show forth this matter as it becomes conscious of its own being and plunges nonetheless desperately into dreams which (it well knows) are nonexistent; singing all the while of our Soul and of all similar and heavenly impressions stored up in us since the earliest times; and, in the face of Nothingness

Which is the Truth, proclaiming this glorious fiction! Such is my volume of poetry and such, perhaps, its title: *The Glory of Fiction* or *Glorious Fiction*. I shall sing it in the tones of my despair.

That is, if I live long enough! Because the other emptiness I found is in my chest. I am really not very well. I can't breathe with ease or with any pleasant feeling of good health. But let's not talk about that. The only thing that bothers me is the thought that, if I have only a few more years to live, I am losing too much time earning a living—so many hours that ought to be devoted to Art, hours that are gone.

What inspirations I would have if only I weren't forced to break up my day like this. I'm stuck with the most stupid profession imaginable—and the most exhausting, too; you would only worry if I were to tell you what a wreck I am after those hoots and spitballs in class. I come out of it all in a stupor. That is why I have taken to working at night, difficult though it is.

To Henri Cazalis, May 12, 1866

I am laying the foundations for a book on Beauty. My mind is moving in the midst of the Eternal and has felt Its waves, if I may so speak of the Immovable. I am relaxing with the composition of three short poems—short but tremendous, all three of them written to glorify Beauty. And when these are tiring, I relax with three very interesting prose-poems. And there you have my summer.

To Henri Cazalis, July, 1866

Yes, I am traveling, but in unknown lands; and if I have fled from the fierce heat of reality and taken pleasure in cold imagery, it is because, for a month now, I have been on the purest glaciers of Esthetics; because, after I had found Nothingness, I found Beauty. You can't imagine the lucid heights that I have dared to climb. Out of this will come a splendid poem that I am working on now; and this winter (or next) will come *Hérodiade*. Without realizing it, I had thrown myself heart and soul into this poem; that was the reason for my doubts and discomforts. But I have finally found the key to it. That is a great comfort, and my great Work will be made the easier on account of it.

To Théodore Aubanel, July 16, 1866

Never in all my life have I worked so hard as this summer; in fact, I have worked *for* all my life. I have laid the foundations for a magnificent work. Every man has his own special secret. Many men die without having discovered it, and they will not discover it because, when they are dead, neither they nor their secret will remain. I died, and I have risen from the dead with the key to the jewelled treasure of my last spiritual casket. Now I shall open it far from all borrowed inspiration, and its mystery will spread through the most beautiful of heavens. For twenty years I shall take monastic refuge in myself, shunning all publicity, except for private readings with my friends. I am working on everything at once; I mean that everything is so well ordered in me that each sensation is transformed at birth and simply pigeon-holed in a given book or poem. When a poem is ripe, it will fall. You can see that I am imitating the natural law.

To Théodore Aubanel, July 28, 1866

I haven't had a moment to explain the enigma of my last letter, and I certainly don't want to *be* an enigma to such good friends as you, even though I sometimes use that way of making other people think about me. . . .

I meant simply that I had just finished planning my entire Work; that I had found the key to myself, the crown, or the center (if you prefer to call it that, so we won't get our metaphors mixed)—the center of myself where, like a sacred spider, I hang on the main threads which I have already spun from my mind. With these—*and at their intersections*—I shall make the miraculous laces which I foresee and which already exist in Beauty's bosom.

I meant that I shall need twenty years for the five volumes of this Work; that I shall be patient and read parts of it to friends like you, and I shall scorn fame as I would any other stupid, worn-out idea. For what is relative immortality—especially since we are often immortal in the minds of idiots—compared to the joy of looking on Eternity and enjoying It within ourselves while we are still alive?

To Villiers de l'Isle-Adam, September 24, 1866

I was dumbfounded by your letter because I really *wanted* to be forgotten; I had intended to be alone in hours of remembrance which even the *Past* itself could not have visited. As for the Future, at least the immediate future, my soul has been destroyed. My thought has gone the limit and thought itself through; it has lost the power to evoke the emptiness spread through its pores and turn it to a matchless Nothingness. Beneath a wave of sensitiveness, I was able to understand the intimate relationship of Poetry to the Universe; and, to make Poetry pure, my design was to divorce It from Dreams and Chance and link It to the idea of that Universe. But, unfortunately, since my soul is made for poetic ecstasy alone, I had no Mind at my disposal (as you have) to clear the way for this idea. And so you will be terrified to hear that I discovered the Idea of the Universe through sensation alone—and that, in order to perpetuate the indelible idea of pure Nothingness, I had to fill my brain with the sensation of absolute Emptiness. The mirror in which the image of Being appeared to me was most often Horror, and you can well imagine how cruelly I am atoning for the precious diamond-light I stole from those indescribable Nights. But I am left with the perfect definition and inward dream of two books, original and yet eternal: one of them a perfect absolute called "Beauty"; the other a personal work called "Sumptuous Allegories of Nothingness." And yet the irony and Tantalian torture is that, if my body is to rise from the dead, I must remain powerless to write them for a long time. For I am in the last stage of nervous exhaustion; my mind is so evilly, so perfectly afflicted that I am often unable to understand even the most banal conversation. And so even this simple, awkward letter I am trying to write you is a dangerous undertaking for me.

Really, I am afraid that I may be *starting* my life with the madness which was the *end* of the great and pitiful Baudelaire —despite the fact that *Eternity* has glittered undeniably in my mind and destroyed whatever sense of Time I may have had.

To François Coppée, December 5, 1866

I have left Tournon for Besançon—an ancient center of war and religion, dark and imprisoning. I have been here a month now. I wonder if I am going to be happy with the change. Up to now, I have been very *un*happy: I've scarcely recovered from all the piddling details involved in a big move, and getting settled, and all the endless *visits* I had to pay stupid officials so as not to get on their wrong side right away. They consider me a somewhat doubtful quantity. (In a few days, I'll tell you why I had to leave Tournon.) Good Lord, what a series of tortures you have to go through to make a living! And even then you don't make it! What drudgery society inflicts on its Poets! . . . My apartment is only half ready as yet. I can't start living again until I get my own room, fill it with my own thoughts, and bulge out the window panes with my inward Dreams, like those richly jewelled drawers of an expensive piece of furniture or tapestries draped in remembered folds. . . .

No successful poem can be written by Chance: that is the central fact which several of us have discovered and proved. I think that once we have perfectly defined poetic form, our principal aim should be to make the words of a poem self-mirroring (since they are sufficiently autonomous to begin with and need no outside impression) to such an extent that no one of them will seem to have a color of its own, and all of them will be merely the notes of a scale.

To Henri Cazalis, May 14, 1867

These last months have been terrifying. My Thought has thought itself through and reached a Pure Idea. What the rest of me has suffered during that long agony, is indescribable. But, fortunately, I am quite dead now, and Eternity Itself is the least pure of all the regions where my Mind can wander—that Mind which is the abiding hermit of its own purity and untouched now even by the reflection of Time. Unfortunately, it was my horrifying sensitivity that brought me to this extremity, and I must veil it over now with outward indifference. That is the only way to recover my lost energy. I achieved a supreme synthesis, and now I am slowly recovering my strength. As you can see, amusement is impossible. And yet how infinitely more impossible it was a few months ago when I struggled with that creature of ancient and evil plumage—God—whom I fortunately defeated and threw to earth. But I had waged that battle on His boney wing, and in a final burst of agony greater than I should have expected from Him, He bore me off again among the Shadows; then victoriously, ecstatically, infinitely, I floated downward until finally one day I looked again in my Venetian mirror and saw the person I had been several months before—the person I had forgotten. I should add—and you must say nothing of this— that the price of my victory is so high that I still need to see myself in this mirror in order to think; and that if it were not in front of me here on the table as I write you, I would become Nothingness again. Which means that I am impersonal now: not the Stéphane you once knew, but one of the ways the Spiritual Universe has found to see Itself, unfold Itself through what used to be me.

So evanescent is my ghostly presence here on earth, that my metamorphoses must be limited to an absolute minimum; otherwise the Universe cannot find Itself in me. Therefore, at this moment of Synthesis, I have outlined the work which is going to be their image: three verse poems, with *Hérodiade* as the overture—poems of a purity which man has never reached and will never reach, perhaps, because I may be simply the victim of an illusion and the human mind may not be perfect enough to convert such ideals to reality. Then I will do four prose-poems on the spiritual idea of Nothingness. I need ten years for all this. Will I live that long?

And now about you. I think your titles and ideas for poems are marvelous. I've gone deeply enough into Nothingness to be able to speak with authority on the subject. The only reality is Beauty and Its only perfect expression is Poetry. All the rest is a lie—except for those who live by the body, by love, or by the mental love that friendship is. . . . Since you are lucky enough to have a love outside of Poetry, then love: doubtless in *you,* Being and Idea will find that paradise which wretched mortals, ignorant and lazy as they are, can only hope to find in death. Then when you think of the nothingness to come, this twin happiness you have found will comfort you, and you will think it all quite natural. As for me, Poetry takes the place of love because it is enamored of itself, and because this self-lust has a delightful dying fall in my soul. But I confess that the Knowledge I have acquired (or rediscovered in the depths of the man I was) would seem insufficient to me—that my entrance into the last Abyss would be a truly crushing blow—if I were not able to finish my work; I mean *the Work,* the "Great Work," as our ancestors the alchemists used to call it.

To Eugène Lefébure, May 17, 1867

My work was created only by *elimination,* and each newly acquired truth was born only at the expense of an impression
which flamed up and then burned itself out, so that its particular darkness could be isolated and I could venture ever more
deeply into the sensation of Darkness Absolute. Destruction was
my Beatrice. I can speak of this now because yesterday I completed the first sketch of my work. It is perfectly outlined; it will
be imperishable if *I* don't perish. I looked upon it without
ecstasy or fear; I closed my eyes and *saw that it existed.*

But I am not proud of this, my dear fellow; in fact, I am rather
sad. For I have not made these discoveries through the normal
development of my faculties, but through the sinful, hasty,
satanic, *easy* way of self-destruction which, in turn, produced not
strength but the sensitiveness that was destined to lead me to
this extreme. I can claim no personal merit in this; on the contrary, it is the fear of remorse (because, impatiently, I disobeyed
the natural law) that makes me take refuge in the impersonal,
as though indulging in a kind of self-vindication.

The most important thing for me is to live with the utmost
care so as to prevent the sickness which, if it comes, will inevitably start in my chest. Up to now, school and lack of sunlight
have been very bad for me; I need continual heat. Sometimes I
feel like going to Africa and begging! When my work is completed, death won't matter; on the contrary, I shall *need* that
rest! Now I must stop, because when my soul is exhausted, I
begin to complain about my body or about society, and that is
sickening.

I think the healthy thing for man—for reflective nature—is
to think with his whole body; then you get a full harmonious
thought, like violin strings vibrating in unison with the hollow
wooden box. But I think that when thoughts come from the

brain alone (the brain I abused so much last summer and part of last winter), they are like tunes played on the squeaky part of the first string—which isn't much comfort for the box; they come and go without ever being *created,* without leaving any trace. For example, I can't recall a single one of those sudden *ideas* I had last year. On Easter day I got a terrible headache from thinking only with my brain, after I had gotten it going with coffee; because it can't get going by itself, and my nerves were probably too tired to respond to any outside impression; I tried to stop thinking that way, and with a tremendous effort I braced the nerves in my chest so as to produce a vibration— still holding on to the thought I was then working on, which became the subject of the vibration, that is, an impression; and so that is the way I am beginning a poem I have been dreaming about for a long time. Ever since then, whenever the crucial hour of synthesis approaches, I say to myself: "I am going to work with my heart"; and then I feel my heart (at those times my whole life is undoubtedly centered in it), and the rest of my body is forgotten, except for the hand that is writing and the living heart, and my poem is begun—*begins itself.* Really, I am shattered. To think I have to go through all that to have a unified vision of the Universe. But if you don't do that, then the only unity you feel is your own existence.

To Villiers de l'Isle-Adam, September 30, 1867

I'll get going again soon on the Poe poems. I accept this task as a legacy from Baudelaire. But not right away . . . because I want to send you a short story in a month or two. I had already made a vague sketch for it, but I was going to put it off for a number of years until I could finish my book on *Beauty.* Its title is: *Bourgeois Esthetics* or *Universal Theory of Ugliness.* So I am going to begin with the part that should have been the appendix, with the *Ugly* rather than the *Beautiful.*

It is simply the symbolics of the bourgeois; what the bourgeois is in relation to the Absolute. He must be shown that he does not exist independently of the Universe (which he thought he could get away from), that he is simply one of Its functions—one of the vilest, in fact. He must be shown what his role is in this Development. If he succeeds in understanding *that,* his joy will be spoiled forever. Don't tell anybody about this work, because I don't want to sell my goods before I have them. It's very hard for me to work, what with being sick, as I am now, and exhausted (as I'm going to be) with the students coming back from vacation—the bourgeois' *sons!* Well, I'll bide my time and be careful; in that way, perhaps, I can get myself into a healthier state of mind. We must drive the monster mad, and I think I have the perfect way to do it.

To François Coppée, April 20, 1868

Your book went straight to my heart and the ecstasy of Poetry —which horrible suffering had long kept in captive sleep—was awakened by this exquisite collection you have written to the glory of verse. Oh, how wise of you to refuse to see anything save through verse alone! For, in these last two years, my sin has been that I have seen my Dream in Its perfect nakedness, when I should rather have veiled It over with mystery, music, and forgetfulness. And now that I have had the horrible vision of a pure work, my reason is almost lost and I have forgotten the meaning of even the commonest words.

To Henri Cazalis, February 4, 1869

The best thing I can do is to repeat your sentence and say that your offer "lifts me back up to the necessary heights"; or rather, lifts me from the *depths.*

Just let me describe the strange state I am in. Immersed and stretched taut in the fulness of the Universe, my thought was in danger of losing its normal function. The mere act of writing gave rise to the most disturbing symptoms. . . .

Now that I have issued a desperate summons to my abandoned will and concentrated my reflective powers in the most solemn way, my heart has returned and taken up the overflow from my thought. Thus my mind has been delivered and will come to itself. You can imagine what a series of unending and infinitesimal efforts this process is going to involve at every minute of the day and night.

But I think there is going to be an inverse proof, as the mathematicians put it: the dream that destroyed me will restore me.

To Henri Cazalis, February 18, 1869

I *had* to stop. My brain was stifled by its Dream and had stopped functioning for lack of any other interest. It would have perished in the midst of its own permanent insomnia. I called upon great Night, Who heard my prayer and spread Her darkness over me. So ended the first phase of my life. Now my consciousness has wearied of the shadows and slowly reawakened. It has fashioned a new man; and when he has been born, he will come again upon his Dream.

To Henri Cazalis, April 23, 1871

In these critical hours, I get glimpses of what my dream has been for these last four years. How near I came to losing it! But now I think I really have it.

But I can't begin working it out right away. First of all, I have to develop the necessary ability and my vision must be ripened, unalterable, and instinctive—as if it had been born long ago and not just yesterday.

Even if I am successful, I'll have to face the fact that it isn't easy to get the general public to accept a work like this. But, after all, it's probably just as well for politics to get along without Literature and decide its fate with guns. That puts Literature on its own.

To Emile Zola, February 3, 1877

This work of yours is truly great, and worthy of an age in which truth has become the popular form of beauty. Those who accuse you of not writing for the people are just as wrong, in a way, as those who are sorry to see you abandon certain ideals of the past. Actually, you have simply invented a modern ideal. The essence of the book is your marvelous experiment with language; this enables you to take over many expressions which are often flat when handled by third-rate writers, and recast them in the most beautiful of literary forms. You succeed in making even writers laugh and cry! I find it all tremendously moving. So far, the beginning of the book is the part I like best: is that just my own inclination or the result of a supreme effort on your part? The tremendous simplicity and sincerity in your descriptions of Coupeau at work or of his wife's garret cast a spell over me which even the gloomy ending couldn't break. We turn the pages of your book as quietly as we live our lives from day to day. You have given something absolutely new to Literature.

To Léo d'Orfer, June 27, 1884

Poetry, when human language has been reduced to its essential rhythm, is the expression of the mysterious meaning of the various aspects of our existence. It therefore gives true value to our life on earth and is the only duty of our soul.

To René Ghil, March 7, 1885

What I particularly like is your attempt (and perhaps you or someone else will bring it off) to lay the foundations of a work from the very start. From this time forward you will know its entire structure. And I admire you for refusing to write unconsciously, however great such works may be.

I am tremendously interested in your attempt at written orchestration. I have only one objection: that even as you are performing that act of justice and restitution which all poets must now perform—that is, recovering everything that Music once took from us: Her rhythms, which are merely those of reason, and even Her colorings, which are nothing but our passions when revery summons them—you tend to let the ancient forms of Verse disappear. The more we extend and rarefy our impressions, the more strictly we must group them in unforgettable, palpable, and strongly accented verses. Yours is the composer's rather than the writer's phrase. I know how exquisite your ideal must seem to you, for it was once my own. But I finally left it, as you may some day of your own accord.

To Gustave Kahn, June 8, 1887

You ought to feel proud! This is the first time in the history of our literature (or of any other, I think) that a poet has abandoned the official rhythm of our language, our time-honored Verse, and created a form of his own—perfect, precise, and enchanting within its own limits. It is really an unheard-of step. The result is that we get a new view of poetry: anyone who has a sense of musical structure can listen to his own particular and inward arabesque of sound; and if he succeeds in transcribing it, he can create his own prosody, apart from the general type which is a sort of public monument in the city of art. What splendid freedom! You realize, of course, that, as far as I am concerned, the new form you have found does not imply the disappearance of the old. The latter will remain impersonal, for it is the property of all poets. Each will have his own way of differing from this norm. What you have done is open a path which is your own. And, what is equally important, you have shown that such paths can be innumerable. The laws you have found in our language are very precise and immediately apparent upon a reading of your work. And they *do exist,* as must countless others which other ears may hear.

To Emile Verhaeren, January 22, 1888

I am also interested in your handling of verse. No one has been more instrumental than yourself in establishing one of poetry's latest and most important conditions. Like a blacksmith, you take your verse from the forge of our time-honored language. You melt it down and give it any form you wish. Sometimes you stretch it out beyond its usual length at the end of a stanza—and even then it is still poetry. Let me congratulate you on that particular point. So it is that the poet disappears (this is without question the great discovery in modern poetry) and the verse itself projects its own passions through its leaps and bounds; its ecstasy lives alone through its own rhythms; and so verse is born, rather than being imposed or brutally thrust upon us by the writer. It all works out beautifully in this poetry of yours. A gleam here or there, a sudden surge of music, begin to create the poem and seem to linger in a hesitating line, like a forgotten sunset cloud. And there are other poems lashed by the torrents of their own storm, eternally, superbly, loudly renewed whenever we dream.

To Henri de Régnier, April 29, 1888

I find the rarest music in these poems of yours. The very subject, with all its feelings and revery, flits and plays on a clear horizon

—and with unbelievable lightness! It has the transparency of the noblest fresco or of orchestral sounds that never quite die away.

To Emile Verhaeren, January 18, 1889

What I admire in your book—and in you, my dear fellow—is the perpetual creation of verses which never lose their fluid quality and yet are always perfectly guided. You don't make the mistake (as poets generally have heretofore) of writing them "once and for all." Rather, they are continually re-created, continually different, and yet still themselves—as life is.

To Jean Moréas, January 5, 1891

Your written melodies seem exquisitely to faint away in voice and coloring, and thus the page you write them on is virginal in the spaces that surround the words. The words themselves— even the most recent of them—imply that you are the only one who has ever spoken them. And surely the chief magic in all this is the particular touch a foreigner gives these Poems in French, while still remaining a son of his own true native land. You do so excellently, and so we come to feel that the language you propose is here forever; that it has, in fact, been the timeless and limitless property and heritage of all poets through the ages.

To Paul Valéry, May 5, 1891

In order to give life and meaning to literature, we must reach that "great symphony." Perhaps no one ever will. Nevertheless, the ideal has obsessed even the most unconscious writers, and its main lines—however gross or fine—are to be found in every written work. The perfect poem we dream of can be suggested by Music itself; and if our own written melody seems imperfect when it has ceased, we must lay siege to the other and plagiarize.

To Vielé-Griffin, August 8, 1891

Thank you for the high ideals you express on my behalf.

Yet everything you say, I have said to myself a thousand times (though less well than you) in the scattered whisperings of my solitude. But where you really divine my thought is in your mention of this very word "is." For that is the title of an interminable study and series of notes I have been working on, and lives in the deepest recess of my mind. There lies the entire mystery: the poet must find and establish hidden identities through a kind of equivalence which will gnaw and reduce physical reality, and always strive for a central state of purity.

To Charles Bonnier, March, 1893

The poetic act itself is this: certain thoughts (which would otherwise remain scattered and distant) are rapidly assembled and arranged in a group of equal and corresponding lines. But, of course, no matter how scattered they may originally have been, they were meant to "go together," so to speak. Therefore their common measure must be established and applied, above all else. The result is Verse. The poem must be brief; then it may multiply and become a book. Its fixed positioning will establish the book's norm, as the verse itself establishes the poem's. Such, at least, is my own vision. On the other hand, I find unique delight in a sort of emotional notation proportionate to the other, yet I enjoy it as prose—a delicate, naked, openwork prose. In this the common measure no longer functions. Either it is totally lacking or else it has no role to play.

To Henri Cazalis, May, 1893

What countless, ancient heavens you have thrilled to! Your verses burst forth with the immediacy of lovely, pure, and lofty inspiration! Those you have just sent me are absolute—definitive creations, unforgettable. And, of course, not a trace of padding around them. It is simply that this kind of verse cannot stand alone, but rather is enveloped by all that vaporous, delicate, and veiled music which it seems suddenly to idealize in moments of intensest heat. We differ, you and I, because you remain faithful to a continual lulling quality in verse which I, in my weariness, tend to neglect. Yet what a miracle it is when it appears essentially, as in your work; when it is truly and eternally magical!

To André Rossignol, May 24, 1893

No, my dear boy, you must not think that you will die, at your age—even if for no other reason than to show Life that It is worth nothing—nothing save what we elicit from ourselves, save what we *are* without Its help.

To Charles Morice, n.d.

I am in complete sympathy with Poe's view that no philosophy, whether moral or metaphysical, must be allowed to appear in a poem. It should not appear, but it should be present and hidden. The scaffolding for the spontaneous and magical architecture must not, of course, be allowed to remain. But this does not mean that powerful and delicate calculations should not enter into the work. It is simply that we must remain unaware of them; they assume an air of mystery of their own accord. Song bursts forth spontaneously from its own native spring—so immaculately that countless rhythmical groups of images are reflected in all directions. What genius it takes to be a poet! What lightning bolts of instinct he must contain! Nothing more nor less than life itself, virginal in its synthesis and all-illuminating. The intellectual armature of the poem must be hidden; it is contained—it *lives*—in the very spaces which isolate the stanzas, and all through the whiteness of the page—meaningful silence which gives no less pleasure in its composition than the verses themselves.

To André Gide, 1897

The poem is now being printed in the form in which I conceived it, including the pagination, which will be its true originality. Certain words in large type will need an entire blank page. I am sure it is going to be very effective. The constellation, obedient to the strictest laws, will move as fatefully as constellations do—at least insofar as it can in a printed book. The ship will heel over from the top of one page to the bottom of the next, and so forth. The big point (which I couldn't explain in a periodical) is that the rhythm of a word group, if it is to make sense, must imitate the action or object in question.

To Emile Verhaeren, April, 1898

I thought I would be seeing your *Dawns* on the Parisian stage this winter. But how glad I am now that the performance will be limited to the spiritual theater within ourselves, where the combination of our inner love of pomp and the splendid vigilance of our thought will present it in its most magnificent form; where our true tragedy lies; where lies the purest, bitterest, and most glorious destiny of each of us. For it is only in that theater that we can have—and truly enjoy as art—the great eloquent exchange of human cries in heavens through which you fly on the extraordinary wings of poetry all your own; for you were the first to give it flight in that fearful, shuddering air.

NOTES

Autumn Complaint

Autumn Complaint first appeared on July 2, 1864, in *la Semaine de Cusset et de Vichy;* then October 27, 1867, in *la Revue des Lettres et des Arts;* February 1, 1872, in *l'Art Libre;* December 20, 1875, in *la République des Lettres;* April 11, 1886, in *la Vogue;* June 26, 1886, in *le Chat Noir;* in *l'Album de Vers et de Prose* (1887); *Pages* (1891); *Vers et Prose* (1893); and *Divagations* (1896).

This prose-poem (originally entitled *The Street-Organ*) was composed in 1864. Having completed his aggressive *Art for All* two years before, Mallarmé now assumed more meditative and reminiscent attitudes. Despite its originality, *Autumn Complaint* makes no attempt to hide its author's acquaintance with Baudelaire's poetry and prose-poetry. In 1862, Mallarmé had undoubtedly read the well-known preface to those prose-poems, in which the author of *Flowers of Evil* had written: "Who of us, in his most ambitious moments, has not dreamed of the miracle of a poetical prose, a musical prose without rhythm or rhyme, yet flexible enough, abrupt enough to adapt itself to the lyrical motions of our soul, to the undulations of our revery, to the sudden fits of our consciousness?" (*Oeuvres Complètes*, ed. de la Pléiade [Paris, 1951], p. 273). Mallarmé took up the challenge; and in *Autumn Complaint* he seems most carefully to have recalled Baudelaire's closing words; for into the midst of this atmosphere of revery steals, indeed, a "sudden fit of consciousness" and of reminiscence—a fit particularly dear to the twenty-two-year-old Mallarmé because it was occasioned by remembrance of his sister Maria, whose death in 1857 had overwhelmed this sensitive and melancholic poet.

Around Maria, restored through memory and forming the autobiographi-

107

cal center of *Autumn Complaint,* Mallarmé weaves his miniature, restless, and ultimately disquieting autumn tapestry. Affection for the fireside, a cat's fur and seemingly mystical presence, poets of decadence, autumnal sensations, the "lust of the mind," languor, and melancholia naturally recall Baudelaire. Yet it is an influence which the receiver has divined from his earliest meditation and totally re-created in his own life and work.

since Maria left me: Charles Mauron, in his fine *Introduction à la Psychanalyse de Mallarmé* (Neuchâtel, A la Baconnière, 1950), pp. 9-44, shows with great insight that the fantastic and lugubrious prose-poem of 1857, *What the Three Storks were saying,* reflects Maria's death and its effect upon the poet.

avenue of poplar trees: here Mallarmé alludes only slightly here to the presence of the city. Elsewhere his prose-poems speak more directly of it, as in *The Demon of Analogy* and *Poor Pale Child,* recalling some of Baudelaire's *Parisian Tableaux.*

The Demon of Analogy

The Demon of Analogy, composed in 1864, first appeared on March 1, 1874, in *la Revue du Monde Nouveau* under the title *The Penult;* then in *le Chat Noir* (March 28, 1885); in *Pages* (1891); *Vers et Prose* (1893); and *Divagations* (1896). For the best analysis, see Albert Thibaudet, *Poésie de Stéphane Mallarmé* (Paris, Gallimard, 1926), pp. 184-88.

This "Chinese puzzle" and "nec plus ultra of the incomprehensible," as Gustave Kahn called it in his *Symbolistes et Décadents* (Paris, Vanier, 1902), p. 138, is the analysis of an obsession which the poet never finally masters. Highly original in tone, style, and treatment, the work was none-theless strikingly foreshadowed by certain passages of Poe's *Berenice:* "My disease," writes Poe's hero, "assumed finally a monomaniac character . . . [which] consisted in a morbid irritability of those properties of the mind . . . termed the *attentive. . . .* To repeat, monotonously, some common word, until the sound . . . ceased to convey any idea to the mind; to lose all sense of motion or physical existence . . . such were a few of the va-garies . . . bidding defiance to anything like analysis."

Mallarmé the poet, teacher, and enemy of Chance in art dwells here—as everywhere—upon the problems of poetry and language, and he tries implicitly to learn and communicate the mechanics of the creative mind—to catch that mind off balance. But all the while, he knows, accepts, and *projects* the ultimate mysteriousness of the process, which accounts for the obscurity and strangeness of his *Demon*. The poet's demon is, of course, the very center of his art—analogy, metaphor, arabesque—and he is therefore haunted not merely by an assemblage of four words but by all the highly unusual associations which they suggest.

sung upon your lips: the reigning analogy of the prose-poem is immediately established: words and music.

strings of an instrument: Mallarmé thinks not of a *piece* of music, but (more unusually) of a musical instrument. Thus the analogy is, at first, visual and seems to be a purely private association. To students of Mallarmean poetry, however, it will recall the exquisite poem *Saint* (1865), in which the poet sets his scene behind a window (presumably some sort of shop-window, similar to the one we find at the end of the *Demon*) and shows a saint surrounded by various stringed instruments. Her wing reminds him of a harp. He then imagines her fingers gliding over the "instrumental plumage," and calls her "musician of silence."

emptiness of meaning: the four words form a run-on line, with the strong syllable *ième* in rhyme position (preceded by the weakly stressed *nul*); the run-on *est morte* provides the "descending tone," and is pronounced as a "dying fall." Appropriately so, in view of the meaning (or meaninglessness) of "The Penult is dead."

the taut string: a string ready to be played upon, inviting the bow. In the same way, says Mallarmé (pursued by his analogic demon), the *nul* sound of *Pénultième* is waiting to be followed or completed by *ième*.

with a palm-branch: now the *nul*, or string, *is* completed, or played upon, by the *ième*, or wing. The wing of memory, he adds, as if to show that *ième* had *remembered* to follow *nul*. The palm-branch is reminiscent of still another poem of 1865, *Bestowal of the Poem*, in which palm-branches, wings, viols, and harpsichords are chief elements.

making them weep: Mallarmé here shows the context of his monomania, i.e., he accounts for the word *Pénultième* by remembering recent grammar lessons wearily expounded to dull students, or linguistic researches of his own which were the necessary but frustrating spade-work for the actual exercise of his "noble poetic faculties."

caressing gesture: before he looked in the mirroring shop-window, Mallarmé had not realized that he was keeping time, with his hand, to his own inner musical mania. Cf. Poe: "[I lost] all sense of motion, or physical existence."

inexplicable Pénultième: is the conclusion of *The Demon of Analogy* merely coincidental, fateful, "supernatural"? Or did the mechanics of the mania lead him "instinctively" down this street and stop him at that particular shop?

The White Water-Lily

The White Water-Lily, composed in 1885, first appeared in *l'Art et la Mode* on August 22 of the same year; then in *l'Album de Vers et de Prose* (1887); *Pages* (1891); *Vers et Prose* (1893); and *Divagations* (1897).

The sheer beauty, delicacy, and syntactical flexibility of the French language have never been more perfectly realized, perhaps, than in this prose-poem. Most of the major Mallarmean themes—absence, silence, dreams, nothingness, metamorphoses of water into mirror, frost, ice, or crystal; the precious treatment of syntax, or a woman's dress, or of her love—all these merge to form the mystery which pervades the poem.

Shortly after he had moved from Avignon to Paris, in 1871, Mallarmé began to spend his summer vacations at Valvins, near Fontainebleau. Here his chief pleasures were his books, his eternal meditation, and the *yole,* or sailboat, in which he idled along the Seine, the better to continue his meditations or to free himself once more from the world of reality. From these excursions came the inspiration for *The White Water-Lily.*

any special landscape: the verdant "ribbon of grass" is not merely a precious substitute for a blade of grass or a reed, but a reminder of the unknown lady's apparel: skirt, lace, and sash. These constitute her charm and therefore a threat to his liberty, just as the ribbon of grass might "hold him near a special landscape," although it does not actually do so until his boat runs into a "tuft" of these ribbons, the "mysterious end of my travels."

watery thicket: an indefinite, small, protective area of the river (centered in the "tuft of reeds") which Mallarmé imagines to be the stage setting of the imaginative adventure soon to come. Generally speaking, it represents the private garden where the poet meditates. Cf. his *Toast Funèbre* (1873).

hesitation of a spring: cf. the hesitation of the elegant lady to that of the elegant pool.

tapering off: i.e., the tops of the reeds, seen in profile from the sailor's vantage point, describe a gentle parabola coincident with, and therefore concealing, the curve of the arch of the bridge that spans the river.

brilliant indiscretion: escape from the brilliance of blue skies was a lifelong obsession which Mallarmé expressed with varying degrees of intensity. Here, the precious treatment is quite in keeping with the spirit of such early poems as *Placet Futile* (1862–87), where the poet renews the tradition of courtly love, or *Autre Eventail* (1887), where the lady finds protection from the heat and light behind a fan. More often, however, the treatment becomes highly serious; Mallarmé seeks protection for himself from the "serene irony of the eternal azure" (*l'Azur*, 1864), preferring night, winter, and cloudy skies, which are more favorable to meditation, so essential to genuine poetic creativity.

familiar with every leaf: an "inner mirror" will protect her from "the brilliant indiscretion of the afternoons." And the poet's imagination finds the method: the "silvery mist" hovering about the river's surface chills the willow trees; these in turn become her mirror and reflect her "limpid glance," which is itself now "familiar with" each mirroring leaf.

cunning twin arrows: i.e., the pointed shoes which know where she wants to go. Mallarmé's interest in women's clothes is best illustrated by the articles he contributed in 1874 to his own short-lived magazine, *The Latest Fashion*.

exquisitely knotted of sashes: this is, of course, the imagined sash—and therefore the most charming or magical. Cf. in *Crisis in Poetry:* "the flower which is absent from all bouquets."

my dream, give counsel: throughout his prose work, Mallarmé makes liberal use of the brief, even the single-sentence, paragraph, with two aims in mind: first, to carry the plot along, as in: "The waiting moment lasts while I decide"; second, to express an exceptionally strong emotion by detaching it typographically, as in: "I conjured her up in her perfection and her purity." The obscure *Coup de Dés* (1897) carries this method to its extreme.

scattered: a favorite Mallarmean word conveying the feeling of vagueness which, to his mind, attaches to absence and, at the same time, is intended to communicate a strong sense of the pervasiveness of that absence. The poet overcomes reality by replacing it with absence, as a body displaces water. Cf. "the scattered walking of many a swan" in *Remémoration d'Amis Belges* (1893?).

flower of my mind: here again the water (in the form of foam making its way to the river bank) may, in devious and Mallarmean ways, become a mirror. But this time, says Mallarmé, it must not, for it would carry with it the image of his "theft," and reveal it to a "chance walker," who might well turn out to be the lady.

executed my plan: in explanation of an early poem, *le Château de l'Espérance,* Mallarmé writes his friend Cazalis: "With military enthusiasm, my heart . . . lays siege to the stronghold of Hope . . . but finds that Hope is only a sort of veiled and sterile specter." (*Ideas on Poetry,* June 3, 1863). In 1885 particularly, with the poems *Quelle soie aux baumes de temps* and *M'introduire dans ton histoire,* as well as in *The White Water-Lily,* Mallarmé pursues the theme of the lover or suitor as military conqueror or knight in the *précieux* world of chivalry and courtly love. Cf. elsewhere in the prose-poem: "the bondage she might lead me into"; the "explorer"; the "imaginary trophy"; and "reconnoitring an estate."

noble swan's egg: bird, wing, fan (which he sees as the bird's wing), harp (considered as an angel's wing)—these are all closely associated in Mallarmé's mind. They are his arabesque of escape, or attempted and frustrated escape. The swan is perhaps chief among these "instruments of magic spells." Cf. *Sainte* (1865), *Remémoration d'Amis Belges* (1893?), *Eventail* (1891), *Autre Eventail* (1887), and *Le vierge, le vivace* (1885).

absence of self: Mallarmé once again attempts to make us feel the reality of emptiness. Cf. *Sonnet* (1887): "Encumbered only with the absence of heavy bouquets."

Glory

Glory first appeared in *les Hommes d'aujourd'hui* in 1886; then on April 7, 1887, in *les Ecrits pour l'Art; l'Album de Vers et de Prose* (1887); *Pages* (1891); *Vers et Prose* (1893); and *Divagations* (1897).

Like *The White Water-Lily,* this prose-poem intensifies a single haunting moment and alternates between the meandering sentence of great beauty and suggestiveness, and the burst of enthusiasm or the clipped, ironical phrase. In both works, the traveler undertakes an inner voyage in search of solitude and ideality, but must first pass through the slough of reality: the ever-present danger of the lady's appearance or the far more present reality of the barking porter and eternal tourists. The reader will decide whether the sharper irony and the closer poet-people relationship of *Glory* make for a successful and integrated two-tone prose-poem, or whether, on the contrary, they contaminate the lyrical quality.

the meaning of Glory: Mallarmé's introduction *("La Gloire, je ne la sus qu'hier, irréfragable")* is a magnificent illustration of the brute or piercing strength of sound which Mallarmean vocabulary and syntax so often provide. Cf. the opening line of *"Victorieusement fui le suicide beau";* and particularly in the *Coup de Dés: "l'Abîme blanchi étale furieux,"* or *"le voile d'illusion rejailli leur hantise chancellera, s'affalera, folie,"* et *passim.*

very borders of the city: the "placards" ("fleeing" away from the train, like telegraph poles) are, of course, "traitors to literature," because they use language for practical purposes. Cf. *The Book: A Spiritual Instrument.*

time of greatness: i.e., autumn, as Mallarmé reveals further on, with its reds and royal purple.

inspired and equalitarian wind: a good illustration of the problem confronting Mallarmé throughout his prose-poem. An inspired wind, yes, since it comes from the mountains; yet equalitarian, he observes with evident irony, since the tourists have as much "right to it" as the poet, even though the latter alone appreciates it. There is really no true equality of feeling.

falling from the boughs of chance: i.e., being metamorphized into poetry. Cf. in *Mystery in Literature:* "The lines of chance vanquished word by word."

trophy too invaluable: cf. in *The White Water-Lily:* "Like an exquisite swan's egg, fated never to burst forth in flight, I carried off my imaginary trophy." So too, in *Glory,* doubt as to the reality of his solitude flies off and leaves behind a trophy, i.e., ecstasy at the thought that he is truly alone now. In his *Après-midi d'un Faune,* Mallarmé wrote: "My doubt, a mass of ancient night, ends up in many a slender branch." There is no great distance, to his mind, between an arm, a wing, and a "slender branch." Each plays a corresponding role in his Ideal.

meaning and reality: this parenthesis, like a musical leitmotif, reminds us of Mallarmé's obsession: the reading and understanding of the natural world, and its re-creation in verse through symbol, synthesis, and idealization.

has only to come: Mallarmé returns here to yet another image group.

Deep colors (here furnished by the autumn season) inevitably lead him on to purple, thence to the idea of royalty, and finally to the poet as prince of beings, watching and hearing nature as a monarch hears his people; celebrating a rite as the monarch holds court. The forest becomes his kingdom; the trees stand like guards bearing torches (i.e., red and yellow autumn leaves) for the royal entrance or "intrusion." For other examples of the torch-purple-royal-prince-hero group, see *La Chevelure* (1887?), *Quand l'ombre menaça* (1883), *Victorieusement fui* (1885), *Quelle soie* (1885), *M'introduire* (1886)—all composed, like *Glory*, in the poet's middle period.

Art for All

Art for All appeared in *l'Artiste*, September 15, 1862, but failed to reappear in subsequent editions of Mallarmé's prose because he judged it unworthy of his maturer prose style.

Unworthy, perhaps; but the essay is blessed with clarity, humor, and enthusiasm from start to finish. The twenty-year-old Mallarmé—more openly passionate here than he will ever be again—outlines his own future attitudes as a poet: saintly obedience to Beauty, which derives additional strength from attacks upon the disrespectful mob.

For a general discussion of the essay, see E. Noulet, *L'Oeuvre poétique de Stéphane Mallarmé* (Paris, Droz, 1940), pp. 37–45.

religious astonishment: Mallarmé's late essays *Catholicism* (1895) and *Sequel* (1895) are notable but obscure treatments of the poetry-religion relationship. Mallarmé considers the poet and priest as ritualists, conjurers; the poet consecrates the alphabet as the priest consecrates bread and wine. See Wallace Fowlie, *Mallarmé* (Chicago, University of Chicago Press, 1953), pp. 231–49.

the greatest of arts: i.e., poetry, of course; but *Art for All* defends all genres; Mallarmé was still to write *Hamlet, Richard Wagner, Music and Literature,* and *Ballets.*

Flowers of Evil: the well-known collection of Charles Baudelaire's poetry which Mallarmé was reading as early as 1861 and which had considerable influence on his own early compositions.

flower-beds: i.e., the columns of a daily newspaper.

Mr. Legouvé's poetry: Ernest Legouvé (1807–1903), minor dramatist, author of *Adrienne Lecouvreur.* His poetry was of the usual academic sort and more immediately accepted than was Mallarmé's.

it is the mob's: Mallarmé's "mob" is usually a vague and vast reading public of average intelligence and little or no patience with poetry, mystery, and allied unrealities. They form the great body of newspaper readers.

"That's for me.": this mildly indignant passage represents Mallarmé at his angriest.

Sanhedrin of art: in Jewish history, a supreme judicial council. Mallarmé is referring here to the elite poets—sole capable judges of things mysterious.

Autobiography

Autobiography, composed on November 16, 1885, was first published in 1924 by Messein. The translation omits the first four paragraphs and the last, which have no general interest.

In 1884, Paul Verlaine had brought out his famous anthology and brief analyses of the *Accursed Poets,* including the names of Verlaine, Tristan Corbière, Arthur Rimbaud, and Mallarmé himself. On November 10, 1885, he wrote Mallarmé requesting biographical information to be used for one in a series of short studies entitled *Men of Today* and published by Léon Vanier. Six days later, Mallarmé complied in the long letter now commonly known as *Autobiography.*

Beckford's Vathek: in 1875, Mallarmé wrote an interesting preface for the reissue of this curious oriental tale written in French by an Englishman.

Etrennes aux Dames: Mallarmé himself wrote a good deal of light verse and remains the undisputed nineteenth-century French master of preciosity.

loving grandmother: Mallarmé fails to mention the more influential death of his sister Maria. See *Autumn Complaint* (notes) and Charles Mauron's *Introduction à la Psychanalyse de Mallarmé.*

Lamartinian: Alphonse de Lamartine (1790–1869), one of the great French Romantic poets.

Béranger's place: Pierre-Jean de Béranger (1780–1857), self-styled "people's poet," as mediocre as he was popular, and an excellent example of the sort of artist that Mallarmé came to scorn as his ideals grew. Cf. the "workers' poet" of *Art for All.*

ambition was too complicated: Mallarmé is being ironical here, of course.

read Poe better: Edgar Allan Poe (1809–49), critic, esthetician, and poet, was one of Mallarmé's chief literary heroes. He translated several of his poems and refers to him in a variety of works, the most famous being the sonnet *Tomb of Edgar Poe* (1876). See, too, the prose piece *Edgar Poe* (1894).

had gotten married: Mallarmé went to England late in 1862 and there married Marie Gerhard, a German school teacher whom he had recently met at Sens, near Paris.

marvelous they may be: for a fuller discussion of this question, see *The Book: A Spiritual Instrument.*

Orphic explanation: Mallarmé was fascinated by Orpheus the enchanter or conjurer (see *Art for All,* notes) who—like the Symbolists—attempts to alter Nature in mysterious ways, even to banish Her and replace Her with Essence.

true function of literature: or, literally, "the literary game par excellence" (*le jeu littéraire par excellence*). Cf. in *Music and Literature:* "Why should we do this? It is a game." Mallarmé saw literature as a game from two essential points of view: first, the elements of literature—words—are always in a dynamic, electric, magnetic relationship. Thus metaphor becomes the soul of poetry. *Crisis in Poetry* is almost wholly concerned with this view: "The poet must establish a careful relationship"; "a volatile scattering"; words are "set in motion as they meet unequally in collision," etc. And in *Mystery in Literature* he describes the "revels of this Language." In short, the game of literature is something infinitely complex, subtle—something infinitely syntactical. Hence Mallarmé's obscurity. But, secondly, although he plays the game more seriously, perhaps, than any other writer, he knows that chance and the infinite are against him. There is a total seriousness to which literature cannot lay claim, any more than all other human endeavors. Hence, broadly speaking, originates his unusual sense of humor and resignation.

equations of this dream, this Ode: see *Ballets* (notes) and the closing pages of *Solemnity* for Mallarmé's interest in number and spirit, and in geometry, rhythm, and structure of the Ode.

Vathek, Raven, Faun: for *Vathek,* see above; the *Raven* is one of Mallarmé's translations of Poe; the *Faun* is the famous *Afternoon of a Faun* composed in 1864–66 and published in 1876.

English Words: a curious and typically Mallarmean study in philology

(1877), ostensibly written as a textbook. Its particular interest lies in the analyses of sensations conveyed by vowel and consonant sounds.

The Ancient Gods: written in 1880 and even more unreadable than *English Words.* It is the Mallarmean version of classical mythology. Both books help to explain Mallarmé's reputation as a poor teacher.

The Latest Fashion: first appeared on September 6, 1874, under Mallarmé's direction—and written entirely by himself. Four months (or seven numbers) later, he abandoned the project entirely. The magazine's lightness and elegance of tone are most reminiscent of the author's occasional verse. The master of preciosity is here at his most precious.

interregnum for the poet: for two reasons: first, as he states here, because his contemporaries had lost sight of the importance of poetry; secondly, because the alexandrine verse had, he thought, reached a stopping-place; it needed a rest; it needed poets who would withdraw to work out their own variations on this metrical theme. In the *Evolution of Literature* Mallarmé notes the advantage of "creating a sort of interregnum for the noble alexandrine which has been at bay, crying for mercy"; and further on: "A poet today, in the midst of this society which refuses to let him live, is a man who seeks out solitude in order to sculpture his own tomb."

they do not exist: a sudden complication of language signals the approach of a Mallarmean irony which is here based on a wilful confusion of two ways of saying "alive." The "living," or *vivants* (i.e., negligible contemporaries, modernists, or even distant friends of the poet), do not really exist, *n'ont pas lieu.* To "take place" (*avoir lieu*) is, in Mallarmean terminology, to live the highest poetical life.

protected by my family: i.e., by his wife (Marie Gerhard) and daughter Geneviève. A son, Anatole, had died in 1879, when only eight years old.

Villiers: Villiers de l'Isle-Adam (1840–89), short-story writer and novelist, undoubtedly the closest of Mallarmé's friends, along with Manet. Following his death, Mallarmé went to Belgium to deliver a lecture on the life and works of his friend; the result was the great essay of 1890, *Villiers de l'Isle-Adam.*

Mendès: Catulle Mendès (1841–1909), very active figure on the French literary scene, had helped Mallarmé in practical ways and had been a good friend as early as 1861. But he was a mediocre poet, as Mallarmé himself confessed in his two-edged compliments in *Ideas on Poetry,* and a man of unpredictable moral sense.

Manet: Edouard Manet (1832–1883), the well-known French Impressionist painter, in whose defense Mallarmé wrote the articles *M. Manet and the Selection* (1874) and *The Impressionists and Edouard Manet* (1876).

Against the Grain: Joris-Karl Huysmans' (1848–1907) best known novel (1884), in which the decadent hero Des Esseintes speaks of the delights and originality of Mallarmean poetry.

regular Mallarmeans: such men as Verlaine, Villiers, or the poet Jean Moréas who, in 1880, first attended the Tuesday evening literary discussions at Mallarmé's home.

place on the edge of the Seine: i.e., Valvins, Mallarmé's summer home. See *The White Water-Lily* (notes).

The Evolution of Literature

This interview—see below—took place on March 14, 1891, and appeared shortly thereafter in the *Echo de Paris*.

Perhaps more accurately than any other of his works, *The Evolution of Literature* evokes Mallarmé's charm and conversational style on those Tuesday evenings when he stood chain-smoking and whispering literary theories in front of the white porcelaine stove at 89 Rue de Rome, *au troisième*. One of the superb conversationalists (or monologuists) of his time (quiet of speech and manner and possessed of a delicate sense of humor), he drew some of the greatest minds to these *causeries:* André Gide, Paul Valéry, Paul Claudel, Paul Verlaine, Paul Gauguin, and Claude Debussy. But no lesson was taught and none of the disciples recorded the master's sayings. Hence the value of *Evolution*.

Early in 1891, Jules Huret, representing the *Echo de Paris*, held interviews in the homes of several of the leading writers of the day: Anatole France; Emile Zola; Maurice Barrès; J.-K. Huysmans; Jules Lemaître; and Paul Verlaine among others. In contrast to the bitterness or meanness of most of the replies, Mallarmé tried merely to explain the aims and heroes of Symbolist poetry. Some of these aims he couched in terms of such concision and power that they count today among the most famous of Mallarmean pronouncements on art.

Stéphane Mallarmé: the short preface to the interview is Huret's. Mallarmé was then forty-nine.

pointed ears: sometimes adduced—even seriously—as reasons for Mallarmé's choice of hero for *The Afternoon of a Faun*.

rhythmical gestures: cf. the "downward and caressing gesture" of the poet's hand in *The Demon of Analogy*.

his own flute: Mallarmé habitually speaks of the poet's "instrument": for Orpheus, the lyre; for the Faun, the flute; for Saint Cecilia, the harp, etc.

organ of official meter: i.e., the classical alexandrine, usually a tetrameter of fairly limited rhythmical possibilities, used almost exclusively in seventeenth- and eighteenth-century French poetry. With the advent of Victor Hugo in the nineteenth century, it underwent profound rhythmical and tonal change. In addition, poets began to abandon it more freely for the decasyllable or octosyllable.

Sagesse: published in 1881 four years before Hugo died. The volume's technical interest lies in Verlaine's use of the five-, seven-, nine-, and ten-syllable verses.

literary manifestations: it is difficult to follow Mallarmé's argument that social disunity could account for the rhythmic dislocation of the alexandrine or for Verlaine's original handling of the seven-syllable verse.

posters and the back page: see *Glory* and *The Book: A Spiritual Instrument*.

crisis moments of the soul: several of Mallarmé's comments in *Evolution* were to be repeated or revised three years later in *Music and Literature*. The 1891 proposition, social disunity means verse dislocation, becomes in 1894: "Governments change; prosody remains ever intact." Cf. too: "As long as there is cadence, there is versification; that is why the careful prose of discriminating writers . . . can always be thought of as broken verse."

broken melodies: Mallarmé is referring here to Impressionism and, in particular, to Claude Debussy who, in 1894, put the broken melodies of *The Afternoon of a Faun* to music in his famous *Prelude* to that poem.

The Parnassians: this school of poetry—including such names as Leconte de Lisle, José-Maria de Hérédia, Léon Dierx, Sully Prudhomme, Théodore de Banville—fits (with much overlapping) between the Romantics and the Symbolists. By "scission," Huret means that certain of the original Parnassians became Symbolists, just as certain of the original Dadaists of our century became Surrealists and Futurists.

majestic first verse: Mallarmé's own poem *Coup de Dés* has thus far been the only outstanding fulfillment of this prophecy.

can be infinitely varied: Mallarmé himself generally remained faithful to the alexandrine. Note that the greatest French poets—Racine, Baudelaire, Mallarmé, for example—were relatively timid innovators.

present things directly: a Parnassian such as Leconte de Lisle paints a "poetic" picture of a panther or an elephant in sometimes dangerously prosaic alexandrines. Mallarmé's quarrel is not with the panther, but with the presentation. The object should rather be suggested, circumvented, somehow made present-absent for us—an admittedly difficult feat where elephants are concerned. Cf. in *Crisis in Poetry:* "We renounce that erroneous esthetic . . . which would have the poet fill the delicate pages of his book with the actual and palpable wood of trees, rather than with the forest's shuddering."

constituted society: society, for Mallarmé, is: first, the hostile, antipoetic mob of *Art for All* or *Mystery in Literature;* second, the vague economic force which makes the poet a "sculptor of his own tomb"; third, the perfect group (in a distant future) which will sit silently at a play, a concert, or a Mallarmean church service, watching the poet (i.e., actor, conductor, or priest) institute "pomp and circumstance." See Wallace Fowlie, *Mallarmé* (Chicago, 1953), pp. 235-41.

"Mendès, Dierx, and Cladel": for Catulle Mendès, see *Autobiography* (notes). Léon Dierx and Léon Cladel were minor poets associated with the Symbolist as well as the Parnassian movement.

with his pride: see *Verlaine.*

didn't belong to her: a slightly involved and precious joke: a common woman who steals precious stones has no right to them on esthetic grounds, since she is unaware of their "secret meaning," i.e., their value, and may well have been at pains to steal the most inexpensive.

Emile Zola: with his numerous and massive novels, his Balzacian energy and pretensions, his sense of the panoramic and historical, Zola stands at the opposite pole from Mallarmé. Was the latter's admiration simply attraction of opposites, like Baudelaire's for Balzac? Note Mallarmé's emphasis on Zola's sense of organization, for which he had great respect.

Morice, Moréas: Charles Morice (1861-1919) and Jean Moréas (1856-1910) were both minor Symbolist poets. Morice is chiefly remembered for his Symbolist manifesto, *Recent Literature* (Paris, Perrin, 1889). Both men were typical of the Tuesday evening disciples.

Henri de Régnier: probably the best of the minor Symbolist talents (1864-1936) and highly representative with his poetic mixture of the exotic, aristocratic, decadent, and languorous. Mallarmé's admiration for his disciples and for many of his *confrères* was often evidence of his politeness rather than of frank literary criticism.

The Book: A Spiritual Instrument

The Book: A Spiritual Instrument first appeared in *la Revue Blanche*, July 1, 1895, and was one of a number of articles by Mallarmé published that same year under the title: *Variations on a Theme*. It next appeared in *Divagations* (1897) as the last of three articles grouped under the subtitle: *Concerning the Book*.

In the ballet, the theater, and in music Mallarmé found facets of his Ideal. But the Book remained the absolute diamond center of his esthetic, balancing and absorbing all other arts. "The Great Work," he exclaims in *Autobiography*, "I mean . . . a book which *is* a book, architectural and premeditated, and not a miscellany of chance inspirations."

The Book makes it clear—in its alternately choppy, ugly, and beautiful prose—that while a book may be a "hymn, all harmony and joy," it has first to be manufactured. Mallarmé brought a good deal of thought and practical sense to bear on this question in connection with the printing of his *Coup de Dés*. Similarly, before it can be a "total expansion of the letter," the book must be word, sentence, paragraph, white page, and "foldings"; hence Mallarmé's obsession with these elements.

Although discussion of the Book is implicit in almost all of Mallarmé's prose, the problem receives special attention in the essays *Limited Action* (1895), *Displays* (1892), and *Crisis in Poetry*.

For detailed discussion, see Guy Delfel, *L'Esthétique de Stéphane Mallarmé* (Paris, 1951), pp. 161–84; Jacques Schérer, *L'Expression Littéraire dans l'Oeuvre de Mallarmé* (Paris, 1947), pp. 200–10; Albert Thibaudet, *La Poésie de Stéphane Mallarmé* (Paris, 1926), pp. 349–63; and L.-J. Austin, "Mallarmé et le rêve du *Livre*," *Mercure de France* (January 1, 1953), pp. 81–108.

author of a statement: see the last sentence of *The Evolution of Literature*.

the unpossessed: cf. in *Autobiography:* "Not that I will accomplish the work in its entirety—it would take a miracle poet to do *that*."

no author's name: cf. in the essay *Whistler:* "A work like his—inborn and eternal—gives the secret of beauty, conjures with the miraculous, and eliminates the signer."

newspaper is the sea: this is a "point of departure," says Mallarmé
literally; a more accurate translation might be "cesspool." But cf. in
Art for All: "The poet . . . is not on a level beneath which other men
crawl; the mob is a level and the poet flies above it."

tomb in miniature: the Book, like the Chimaera (see *Richard Wagner,*
notes), is the simultaneous source of beauty and death. The creator of
beauty "goes into isolation to sculpture his own tomb," says Mallarmé
in *Evolution.* Contrast in *The Theater and Recent Dramatists* (1886):
"The superimposition of pages, like a casket which protects against
unfeeling space the folded, infinite, intimate delicacy of Being in
Itself."

at its foundation: cf. Mallarmé's *Mourning* (1893): "For a long time, the
traditional *feuilleton* on the ground floor upheld the whole mass of
the format. . . . Now, things are better: true fiction . . . flutters across
the 'daily papers' and alights triumphantly at the most important
points—and even at the top."

wings in repose: flight is, of course, the leitmotif of *The Book:* the
newspaper fluttering over the roses, the book-bird's "foldings," the
white butterfly in the last paragraph. Mallarmé returns time and
again to this theme.

mass production: in his essay *Displays,* Mallarmé remarks: "The open-air
edition bursts its bonds to fit the gloved hand of a woman on her
travels. She quickly chooses a pamphlet so that she will be able to
place it between her eyes and the ocean."

twenty-four letters: cf. in *Music and Literature:* "Perfect reverence for
the twenty-four letters of the alphabet. These he shall transform,
through the miracle of infinity . . . and will then possess . . . a principle for knowledge."

inherent in its structure: the relationship of printed words to blank
spaces determines the lasting architecture of the Mallarmean Book.
Cf. in *Ideas on Poetry:* "The intellectual armature of the poem must
be hidden; it is contained—it *lives*—in the very spaces which isolate
the stanzas, and all through the whiteness of the page—meaningful
silence which gives no less pleasure in its composition than the verses
themselves." Thus, format and content are inextricably related.

lightning-like initiative: hardly sufficient in itself for the learning of
Mallarmean syntax, for example.

ancient times to bleed: for the psychological implications of this and
the following sentence, see R. G. Cohn, *L'Oeuvre de Mallarmé* (Paris,
1951), p. 151 (notes). See also: Charles Chassé, "Les Thèmes de la
Stérilité et de la Virginité chez Mallarmé," *Revue des Sciences Humaines* (April–June, 1953), pp. 171–81.

scattering of ornaments: this passage serves as an accurate description

of Mallarmé's own *Coup de Dés,* composed two years after *The Book.*
See in *Ideas on Poetry* the letter to André Gide, 1897.

white butterfly: returning again to the opening scene of his essay,
Mallarmé attempts a subtle closing thought. Is the butterfly simply the
original newspaper which started him off on his meditation? Thibaudet
seems to think so (*op. cit.,* p. 356), although it would seem to be a
rather gentle name for an object so distasteful to the poet. And yet,
if so, the sentence is more readily explained: the sharpness and frankness of Mallarmé's ideas will flit like a butterfly, i.e., like or in a newspaper (or in *la Revue Blanche*) before its amazed (i.e., irritated)
readers.

Mystery in Literature

Mystery in Literature is the last of the *Variations on a Theme* which Mallarmé composed, for the most part, in 1895. It first appeared in *la Revue
Blanche,* September 1, 1896; then in *Divagations* (1897).

Distinctly less clear than its nearest contemporary, *Verlaine,* this essay
is made up (like *Solemnity*) of two elements: irony and poetic theory.
Typical of Mallarmé's final prose manner, its frequent and majestic
beauties seem nonetheless strange and sometimes disorderly—syntactically
tortured into life. The champion of mystery at once seeks and shuns his
Mob, with the result that in style and attitude the work remains paradox-
ical throughout.

> *cannon fodder:* the aggressive tone of the essay is immediately
> established.
> *lending out their language:* cf. in *Music and Literature:* "Infinity—
> Whose rhythm . . . can be rendered by the fitting words of our daily
> tongue."
> *their first impression:* Mallarmé hints, in passing, at his central idea that
> the seemingly unintelligible and unpopular work does, in fact, apply
> to the "idlers," who will later be called "the vessel of Genius."
> *no hard feelings:* half-amused, half-bitter acceptance of the eternal dif-
> ference and misunderstanding between artist and idler.
> *disquieting gleam:* i.e., despite its obscurity, the Mallarmean poem (or
> any great work) has some secret power of radiation to which even the

common eye is not insensitive. Thus the poem is nearer to the life and dreams of Everyman than Everyman is willing to admit. Poetry does not have a language all its own.

She sniffs out: cf. Mallarmé's *Art for All:* "The barking sounds of a pursuing pack of creatures."

anything but Herself: the Mob has now become a shrew; in passages to follow, She will be a prostitute driven on and "satisfied" by idlers and "fellow citizens."

a Nightless well: i.e., a well without mystery, therefore useless to literature.

vessel of Genius: the sexual overtones of the "inkwell," the "vessel," and further on the "lacuna" and "dehiscence" certainly cannot be denied.

Our Lady: through this quite frank and mocking language Mallarmé is defining the Mob as the poet's muse: he uses her language and writes for her, whether she knows it or not. This is a recurring paradox in Mallarmé.

broken glass: this is surely one of the strangest of all Mallarmé's images, despite its brutal effectiveness and the vague symmetry of leisure and headaches, vertical flowers and plaster images, fountains and broken glass (for the metamorphoses of water, see *The White Water-Lily*), greenery and green bottle bottoms.

Music came along: there is no discursive reason for the isolation of this paragraph (or for several other single-sentence paragraphs in this essay), since it is merely the conclusion of the preceding. But Mallarmé evidently considers that the introduction of Music deserves special treatment.

musical veils: veils, "motifs," "triumphant bursts," and "essential brilliance" recall Mallarmé's vision of Wagner. Cf. the "deity draped in the invisible folds of a musical texture" in his *Richard Wagner, Revery of a French Poet.* Mallarmé demonstrates here the methods and lessons which literature can learn from music, especially that of the opera or ballet.

essential brilliance: cf. this paragraph with the following one from *Music and Literature:* "Certain orchestral phrasings in which we hear, first, a withdrawal to the shades, swirls and uneasy hesitation, and then suddenly the bursting, leaping, multiple ecstasy of Brilliance, like the approaching radiance of a sunrise."

repertory of nature: cf. in *Music and Literature:* "symphonic equation of the seasons of the year."

Syntax: a separate whole paragraph is naturally devoted to the one word which describes the artist; it also lies in pleasing contrast to his earlier quip: *"Their* undertaking."

its knowing transpositions: this sentence, too, is reminiscent of *Music and Literature* where Mallarmé defines the soul as a "knot of rhythm" and describes the actions of the Monster-Poem.

walls of a cave: in his essay *Igitur*, Mallarmé speaks of "gleaming walls" mirroring the hands of the hero. Here he may mean the walls as dark, parallel lines (i.e., of verse) which, like mirrors, "exchange their brilliancies."

wedding of the Idea: in this unusually beautiful paragraph, the "halves of whiteness" would seem to be the blank space on the page following the poem (i.e., the "silence genuine and just") and the lucidity, transparence, or whiteness of the good reader's vision. In silence and solitude the two mysteriously meet—this being one aspect of the mystery of literature—and the wedding is accomplished which makes them One, i.e., produces the Idea. For further comment on the passage, see R. G. Cohn, *L'Oeuvre de Mallarmé* (Paris, Librairie des Lettres, 1951), p. 151 (notes) and Charles Mauron, *Introduction à la Psychanalyse de Mallarmé* (Neuchâtel, A la Baconnière, 1950), p. 197. See, too, a different and excellent interpretation in Gardner Davies, *Vers une Explication rationnelle du "Coup de Dés"* (Paris, Corti, 1953), pp. 49–50, according to which the halves of whiteness are the blank spaces before and after "the lines of chance have been vanquished," that is, Hegelian opposites which are synthesized in the Idea.

Crisis in Poetry

The translation includes all but the first three paragraphs of *Crisis in Poetry*. The essay consists of the following: paragraphs 1–3, from the beginning of the essay *Averses ou Critique* which appeared in *la Revue Blanche*, September 1, 1895; paragraphs 4–17 (ending with: "free and individual modulation"), from the essay *Vers et Musique en France* in *The National Observer*, March 26, 1892; paragraphs 18–27 (ending with: "could not be properly closed"), from *Averses ou Critique;* paragraph 28, from *Music and Literature;* paragraphs 29–31, from *Vers et Prose* (1893); paragraph 32 (ending with: "passionate control of verse"), from *Vers et Musique en France;* paragraphs 33–34, from *Averses ou Critique;* paragraph 35, from *Vers et Prose;* and the remainder, from Mallarmé's preface (or *Avant-Dire*) to René Ghil's *Traité du Verbe* (1886).

Despite its structural weakness, occasional repetitiousness, and largely unvarying seriousness, *Crisis in Poetry* stands with *Music and Literature* as the greatest and most beautiful of Mallarmé's pronouncements on poetry. For sheer variety, it is unequalled in his criticism: all the leading Mallarmean leitmotifs are present—lightning, fire, jewel, temple, veil, arabesque, Chimaera, and flight—together with discussions (or concise definitions) of poetic evolution and *état présent*, and structure of verse, strophe, and volume.

upheaval: Mallarmé is here referring to the beginnings of Romantic poetry.

temple's veil: see *Solemnity*.

death of Victor Hugo: in 1885, the very year in which Symbolism and Mallarmé were beginning to achieve some measure of celebrity in literary circles.

poetry personified: cf. in *Evolution:* "I am sure that when Hugo died, he was convinced that he had buried all poetry for the next century." In *Crisis,* Mallarmé's irony is more veiled, but still present. Hugo's reduction of prose genres to poetry was hardly to be admired by the Mallarmé who agreed with Poe that "Beauty is the province of the poem."

we have verse: cf. in *Evolution:* "Poetry is everywhere in language, so long as there is rhythm."

freely scattering: because the common alexandrine could be a heavy, boring, albeit indestructible whole, lacking in rhythmic imaginativeness, Mallarmé's descriptions of modern verse emphasize flexibility and inner breaks, scatterings, sparklings, and elements soaring individually like shrapnel, bursting rockets, and musical notes.

take great interest: for a truer, less modest definition of Mallarmé's role, see *Evolution, Autobiography,* and the essay *Solitude* (1895).

magic power: cf. in *Solemnity* rhyme's "sudden fluttering and rise from earth."

reveal the weft: see *Autobiography* and, in *Music and Literature,* Mallarmé's note: "I have neither blame nor disdain for ecliptic periods in art; even then art is instructive, for its wear and tear serve to reveal the sacred manias of the weft."

abstinence from theft: cf. in Mallarmé's *Evolution:* "We say to children: 'Don't steal, and you'll be honest.' That is true, but it is not everything."

twelve tones: i.e., the twelve syllables of the alexandrine. The "mechanisms" and "metronomes" are the hemistiches and other regularizing metrical divisions.

Henri de Régnier: see *Evolution* (notes).

sword or flower: used here because they are symbols of national celebration.

Jules Laforgue: (1860–87), one of the most original, ironical, and sensitive of the late nineteenth-century French poets. His thought and technique alike have had considerable influence on T. S. Eliot and Ezra Pound, among others.

pedants: the pedants, of course, were the Parnassian poets who, in 1876–77 (i.e., "fifteen years ago," since this part of *Crisis* was written in 1892), were outraged by Mallarmé's own *Afternoon of a Faun* (see *Evolution*). Note that, throughout *Crisis*, Mallarmé prefers endless variations on the traditional alexandrine to totally new innovations in verse form.

Moréas: see *Evolution* (notes).

Vielé-Griffin: see *Ideas on Poetry* (notes).

Gustave Kahn: (1859–1936), famous for "inventing" free verse in French poetry, he was one of the first members of Mallarmé's Tuesday evenings.

Charles Morice: see *Evolution* (notes).

Emile Verhaeren: (1855–1916), Belgian poet of exceptional power and beauty, contemporary of the Symbolist movement, in sympathy with it, but living outside it.

Edouard Dujardin: (1861–1949), founder of the *Revue Wagnérienne* (1885), to which Mallarmé contributed his *Richard Wagner, Revery of a French Poet.*

Albert Mockel: (1866–1945), minor Belgian poet and critic whom Mallarmé thought promising.

its strands: cf. the metaphors in *Music and Literature:* "Thyrsus of infinite complexity" and "Every soul is a knot of rhythm." The binding up of the soul's melodic strands is a variation on the arabesque theme. It is as if verses still unborn in the poet's mind were straggling threads; composition will realign them or knot them with mental discipline. Cf. the "sacred manias of the weft" (see above) and the following from *Ideas on Poetry:* "Like a sacred spider . . . I shall make the miraculous laces which I foresee."

compared to the opacity: the French words *ombre* and *ténèbres* both mean "shadow" or "darkness." Onomatopoetically, *ombre* (with its dark nasal *om*) seems to fit darkness, while *ténèbres* (with its sharp *é*) seems too bright—although it could well be argued that the *èbres* element brings the word back into the shadows. Similarly *jour* should supplant *nuit* because the sound of its *ou* is darker than the short, piercing, triumphant *i*.

if our dream were fulfilled: i.e., if each word were perfect, there would be no need for word combinations.

hear undeniable rays: in this typically Mallarmean synesthesia, rays of light (i.e., verses) are naturally *heard,* but they also "gild and pierce" a river of song flowing from an orchestra, as a summer sun dances through the rippling sounds of a brook.

distilled and caught: this is one of Mallarmé's finest definitions of Symbol and Idea.

certain masterpieces: e.g., the novels of Zola which Mallarmé particularly admired.

from point to point: cf. in Mallarmé's *Music and Literature:* "The omnipresent Line which runs infinitely from point to point, in its creation of Idea."

square measurements: in *Un Coup de Dés* Mallarmé avoids these scrupulously.

the very silence: the *quality* of silence, Mallarmé implies, will change in accordance with the quality, meaning, or sound of words which are typographically near to a given blank space on the page. This is an excellent example of the hypersensitive or decadent esthetic ridiculed by Marcel Proust through the little speeches and reveries of a Legrandin.

creation of many poets: see *Autobiography.*

Chimaera: see *Richard Wagner* (notes).

flash of lightning: cf. in *Ballets:* "Nameless, impersonal, glittering glance of absoluteness, like that lightning which has . . . enveloped the ballerinas."

Music and Literature

Music and Literature was first published in 1895 by Perrin. It first appeared in October 1894 in *la Revue Blanche* under the title: "Lecture in Oxford and Cambridge."

The essay was preceded in the Perrin edition by a shorter work entitled *Déplacement Avantageux,* or *Prosperous Trip,* which first appeared in *le Figaro,* August 17, 1894, under the title *Le Fonds Littéraire,* and then in *la Revue Blanche,* October 1894. Although *Prosperous Trip* is mainly concerned with the question of public domain in literature, it begins with the author's impressions of England and therefore seems a proper preface to *Music and Literature.*

It will be recalled from *Autobiography* that Mallarmé first went to London in 1862. He was to be an English teacher, profoundly (if somewhat eccentrically) interested in English words and syntax. Oxford and Cambridge, where he delivered his lecture on *Music and Literature,* stood in his mind as symbols of the poet's paradise. In *Prosperous Trip* he speaks enthusiastically of their "communion in study . . . the Tudor atmosphere refreshed by the air of meadows . . . the stags and running waters"; and from a reading of the following passage we can judge how thoroughly at home the unhappy teacher of high-school language would have felt in such surroundings and seclusion, in these "twin marble citadels in flower, constructed for thought."

"It is all eminently simple: youth entrusts its growth to the sheltering architecture of these sites of thought; and there, nearby, is the gentle presence of older men renowned throughout Europe and the entire world. To them, I think, these historiated stones are specially dedicated, as is my own interest here. They live and work today for the sake of beauty and perfection—such is the chosen task of this élite whom we call *Fellows.*"

He goes on to admire the unparalleled and attractive freedom in such scholars' lives: sees them sitting quietly in their libraries, in meditation at their "daily windows," or traveling occasionally on the continent, it being always understood that they shall live monk-like "within these monasteries of knowledge," and receive all aid and attention—save that of "adversity," he adds with a wry smile remembering the case of Verlaine as well as his own. Mallarmé was never reticent about the need for ivory towers or the spiritual superiority of a very few men who should be content with the humblest and most ascetic of lives but demand, in exchange, the privilege of solitude. "When I arrived," he writes, "I became aware of a Past enriched by the seasonal renewal of sunsets soon to come. These things are eternal; so, too, the idea of Cloisters. But to Democracies it is all repugnant: their instinct is to abolish, deny, or tear down. I insist on the word 'Past'— it is our great solace and a lesson to us no less noble than some choir which will sing forever. . . . I wonder, then, whether such institutions as these, impervious to the brutality which would destroy their walls, do not quite simply *abide*—whether they are not *of all time.* Yes, I wonder whether those Gothic works surging spiritually to heaven—that basilica of "Jesus" yonder or this vigilant tower of "Magdalen"—do not rise up from ancient time and go straight on with a will into the future."

It is not surprising, then, that Mallarmé accepted the joint invitation of Charles Bonnier (see *Ideas on Poetry,* notes) and York Powell (see below) to speak in Oxford and Cambridge on the subject of French literature. On May 20, 1893, he writes Bonnier: "Let me thank you [for your flattering invitation]. I want to find a title for my lecture soon (the subject, of course, I don't have to find: it is always the same one with me): perhaps I can call it *Letters and Music*. I will be relaxing in the Fontainebleau forest for a few days now, and I will be able to give it a little more thought. Just between us, could you tell me whether any financial arrangements are involved? Of course, the lecture is sufficiently attractive on its own account."

On March 1, 1894, Mallarmé spoke at Oxford; the following day, at Cambridge. In his *Vie de Mallarmé*, Mondor quotes letters in which Mallarmé dwells interestingly on the circumstances of these talks and on his own impressions: "Oxford is a miracle: over twenty cloisters in the exquisite Medieval style, and parks and pools all around; there is the city, too, and people around, but you soon forget them. Outside my window I have meadows with cows and stags grazing; age-old trees. . . . I did a lot of visiting yesterday . . . and ate in the beautiful dining hall; it is like a cathedral. . . . Here is the menu I stole. Then, I spent an hour in the main room where the professors drink wine and relax without their dining robes."

"I left Oxford today (March 2). Mr. Powell is a fine person. He took perfect care of me. Last night there was a big dinner in my honor. It was marvelous, except for the champagne, the sherry, and the water which don't agree with me at all. I have just now had dinner with Payne: I drank my first beer and liked it a lot. . . . But, Lord! the lecture! If I had only known! Only two or three professors in the audience, a few students, and all the rest were ladies. I can't really complain, though; they were all scrupulously polite, they applauded for a decent length of time, perhaps a little artificially when it was all over. I am the one who is in the wrong: I never should have served up a dish of tough esthetics like that; I could have just chatted with almost no preparation at all. . . . It is a shame that I had to come so long a way and take so much trouble just to provide relaxation for fifty or sixty people who enjoy studying or who want to have a chance to hear French spoken."

"I arrived in Cambridge today (March 3) feeling a little glum because I knew . . . there wasn't much I could expect as far as money was concerned. . . . But the lecture was a different matter. . . . I have never given a lecture—and doubtless I never will again—which so touched me with the sense of exquisite beauty. I never dreamed it could be so. The twenty members of the audience (two of them ladies) formed a perfect élite, friendly and yet discreet. They listened with scrupulous attention, sympathetically, and intelligently. The setting was exquisite. A splendidly panelled room, with beautiful furniture, in Pembroke College. It was nine o'clock in the evening; the audience sat in the shadows: just a table or two with a few candles. And there was daddy standing in front of *his* table in the light of two tall silver candelabra. The applause when I entered and when I left was genuine."

To that extent, undoubtedly, Mallarmé was sensitive to his listeners' response. But he was probably quite unaware of the fact that they understood hardly a word of what he was saying.

Music and Literature is Mallarmé's last will and testament in prose, and certainly his greatest and most comprehensive work in that genre, crystallizing as it does the chief esthetic views expressed in *Crisis in Poetry, Mystery in Literature, Evolution,* or *Solemnity.* From the stylistic point of view alone, its variety, power, and beauty mark it as one of the monuments of the French language. A lifetime of stylistic innovation and refinement is here synthesized: Mallarmé's curious paragraphing technique, the abstract passage, the explosive short sentence, the brilliant image; the *précieux* alternates with the colloquial phrase, the consciously ugly with the beautiful.

I am with you now: in a brief preface to his essay *Music and Literature,* Mallarmé explains: "The Taylorian Association was undertaking a series of lectures by foreign—and particularly French—men of letters. I shall never forget the great honor it was for me when the Christ Church historian (and now my dear friend) York Powell graciously invited me to participate. The evening before my talk, he was kind enough . . . to read his admirable translation of it. . . . The success of the undertaking was thenceforth assured; the word was spread. And the interest which was shown the following evening when I delivered my talk in person was undoubtedly due to Mr. Powell's efforts, which were still fresh in the mind of my listeners." Frederick York Powell (1850–1904) was regius professor of modern history at Oxford and a friend of certain Symbolist poets such as Verlaine and Verhaeren. He had taught Old French at Christ Church College.

my native tongue: it had been originally suggested that Mallarmé deliver his talk in English. But since it had been prepared in French with an obvious view to its permanence as a work of art, he naturally declined.

unexpected heights: in the first of a brief series of *Notes* later appended to the first edition of this essay, Mallarmé contrasts England and France with Italy and Spain: the literary heritage of the former is an "assemblage," whereas a Dante or a Cervantes "reach unexpected heights" totally unapproachable by minor talents.

princely instincts: cf. what Mallarmé says on this in the Fontainebleau forest (*Glory*).

governments change: see *Evolution* (notes).

as broken verse: see the first half of *Crisis in Poetry.*

thyrsus: a variant on the more important arabesque theme. Cf. the web spun by the "sacred spider" in *Ideas on Poetry.*

point of separation: in his *Notes* Mallarmé continues: "Verse shoots forth like arrows [cf. in *Crisis in Poetry:* "We now *hear* undeniable rays of light, like arrows gilding and piercing the meanderings of song."], not so much in succession as almost simultaneously, in order to create Idea. It reduces duration to the spiritual space which the subject naturally demands. Thus it differs from the temporal phrase or development which is prose."

two separate wholes: cf. in Mallarmé's *Crisis in Poetry:* "Poetry, I think, waited . . . until this giant . . . had disappeared; then verse broke up."

knot of rhythm: cf. the thyrsus and the "meshes of a couplet" mentioned further on; and: "Each soul is a melody; its strands must be bound up" (*Crisis in Poetry*).

provide much-needed rest: this idea is often re-echoed in *Crisis in Poetry* and *Evolution.* And in his *Notes* he adds: "So ends, suddenly, the Parnassian dream; the alexandrine has found its inner liberty: complete freedom with the caesura and the hemistich. The Parnassians were condemned because they instituted a self-spoken verse in which the reader's innate sense of song could not participate; it lived by virtue of the position and dimensions of its words. They were behind the times because, although the mechanics of such a verse were very nearly perfect, its purpose and poetics had not been defined. . . . But the real fault, in my opinion, was their intent to express the palpable aspect of things."

should be used sparingly: in Mallarme's *Notes:* "I have neither blame nor disdain for ecliptic periods in art; even then art is instructive, for its wear and tear serve to reveal the sacred manias of the weft." Thus, while he was thought by many to be a poetic revolutionist, he was basically a traditionalist in matters of form.

universal musicality: this passage is of course Mallarmé's answer to the question: "Is there a reason for writing at all?" At the same time, it is one of the most succinct yet comprehensive definitions of Symbolism: distill the material world, volatilize it; do not reproduce it (e.g., Realism, Naturalism), because the Creator has done that for us; then set this nothingness to perfect music. The poet should deal only with the essence of the material world.

struggle with the Ideal: hence we see Mallarmé's frequent identification of the Ideal with a Chimaera.

art of etching: Mallarmé approved classical syntheses and refinement, but disapproved their application to moral and psychological problems.

if they questioned: Mallarmé's own deep questioning resulted finally in the loss not of efficacy, but of quantity.

content to wreathe: cf. in *Ideas on Poetry:* "For in the last two years, my sin has been that I have seen my Dream in Its perfect nakedness, when I should rather have veiled it over with mystery, music, and forgetfulness."

symphonic equation: see *Ballets* (notes).

truly polished: the *précieux* reappears. The truly great poet, in Mallarmé's scheme, is naturally a gentleman, the highest form of civilization. Though suggestive of Baudelaire's dandyism, Mallarmé aims at an even higher refinement.

own virtual power: cf. in *Crisis in Poetry:* "If the poem is to be pure, the poet's voice must be stilled and the initiative taken by the words themselves, which will be set in motion as they meet unequally in collision."

books of magic: i.e., the *grimoire,* a favorite theme which occurs notably in the poem *Prose pour des Esseintes* (1884).

must not, satisfy us: Mallarmé says in *Mystery in Literature:* "I shall simply observe that several of my contemporaries don't know how to read. The newspaper, yes; they can read that. . . . Reading is an exercise." The "manufacture of happiness" refers to typography, page-settings, etc. (see *The Book*).

something else: this brief, powerful paragraph is an admirable illustration of Mallarmé's stylistic obsessions: key words from his vocabulary—*épars* (chance or scattered), *frémissement* (trembling), *surseoir* (suspend, postpone)—are linked together by negatives or syntactical hesitations: the negative *ne,* the subjunctive *veuille,* the conjunction *ou.* The closed or negative quality is further assured by the "something else" which begins, ends, and therefore permeates the paragraph. Cf. the dancer in *Ballets* who "with a touch of her fingers, just before she took a step, would call a shimmering fold forth from her skirt and seem to fly up to the Idea on impatient wings."

thunderbolt height: cf. in *Solemnity:* "Every page . . . announces (these laws), shoots them high to heaven," and the "magnificently illuminated sky of ecstasy." The thunder and lightning themes are frequent in *Music and Literature.*

it is a game: a single paragraph here, of course, since a standard Mallarmean definition of poetry is involved, repeating the famous sentence from *Autobiography:* "The Orphic explanation of the Earth, which is the poet's sole duty and the true function of literature [literally: the literary game *par excellence*]."

sublime attraction: in his *Notes* Mallarmé continues: "My point of view is pyrotechnic as well as metaphysical. For when fireworks reach the height and nature of thought, they can illuminate pure joy." Cf. the *Edgar Poe* of 1894: "I knew the marble forehead; the eyes as deep as stars, if not so distant; the mouth knotted by every serpent save that of laughter. But now, to see the full-length daemon! With his dark

tragic coquetry, restless and discreet. . . . But despite all the daguerro-
types and engravings, some special unprecedented reverence bids me
think only of the purest of Minds—an aerolith star- and lightning-born,
hurled down to us from afar by finite human design, and bursting into
the jewels of a crown to be worn by no one in many and many an age
to come. Truly, *he* is that exception and the absolute model of the
Writer."

Nature exists: cf. in *Evolution:* "Things already exist; we don't have to
create them; we simply have to see their relationships."

in its absence: cf. in *Crisis in Poetry:* "The poet must establish a careful
relationship between two images, from which a third element, clear
and fusible, will be distilled and caught by our imagination"; or:
"Song, when it becomes impalpable joy, will rise to heaven"; or: "Divorce the object from the direct and the palpable, and so conjure up
its *essence* in all purity"; and in *Evolution:* "To *name* an object is
largely to destroy poetic enjoyment."

we conjure up: as the hero of *The Afternoon of a Faun* conjured up his
evanescent and (sensually) "intersecting" naiads.

we recognize: here begins one of the most magnificent passages in
Mallarmé: syntactically bold yet generally clear; highly elliptical ("*La
totale arabesque . . . a de vertigineuses sautes en un effroi que recon-
nue*"); tonally and onomatopoetically powerful ("*Quelle agonie aussi
qu'agite la Chimère versant par ses blessures . . .*"). His arabesque
springs to life, puts on the form of the Chimaera (see *Richard Wagner*), "leaps dizzily in fear," and yet remains perfectly controlled, harmonious within itself. Thus the Poem-Monster-Idea combines a perfectly dynamic state with the perfect calm and omnipresent form of
things classical.

Him Who once unleashed Infinity: is admired only for that quality of infiniteness which lends itself to the Mallarmean arabesque.
Likewise, in *Ideas on Poetry*, when Mallarmé thought that his own
mind had understood infinity, he could say, in effect, that he had no
further use for infinity, that he had "struggled with that creature of
ancient and evil plumage—God—whom I fortunately defeated."

our daily tongue: in *L'Expression littéraire dans l'Oeuvre de Mallarmé*
(Paris, 1947), Jacques Schérer shows that Mallarmean vocabulary was,
in the main, far from esoteric and, upon occasion, extremely colloquial
or even vulgar.

what is Literature: i.e., writing crystallizes, verifies thought; thought thus
vindicated contents the soul and so identifies it with the object of
thought itself.

never very confiding: one of the curious aspects of Symbolism was its simultaneous need for, and distrust of, music. Mallarmé in particular wanted music for the new poetry, appreciated its qualities in the abstract, yet could not accept its apparent imprecision. To him who claims "reverence for the twenty-four letters of the alphabet," the verbal phrase seems more explicit and more palpable than the musical; he is ultimately unwilling to pledge equal allegiance to several modes of expression. That is why Mallarmé found himself in the somewhat false position of wishing to "recover everything that Music once took from us: Her rhythms, which are merely those of reason and even Her colorings which are nothing but our passions" (*Ideas on Poetry*), and, at the same time, of refusing the total *musical effect* of such means. In short, he was not a musician and therefore could not meet music on its own ground. Which explains why, in his musical need, he turned to Wagner who had himself sought to merge the dramatic art with his own musical dreams. A Bach, a Mozart, who (relatively speaking) observed the laws of music for pure music's sake, could offer the Symbolists no technical foothold; their rhythms are not "merely those of reason," their colorings not merely "our passions," but an integral part and projection of the musician's art. It is strange that Mallarmé, the purest of artists in his own *métier* (aware, for example, that his own lyrical and immaculately poetic *Faun* was not "playable on the stage," as he says in *Ideas on Poetry*), did not always make these distinctions. Nonetheless, he did come to feel the inapplicability, to his own genius and to the essential quietness and abstractness of Symbolism, of the highly colored, openly sensuous, and somewhat noisy art of Wagner. Cf. in *Mystery in Literature:* "Yes, the supreme . . . musical moments . . . [are] more true, more central, more brilliant than any reasoning. . . . We feel unable to translate them into any language." Yet, even so, he quickly returns to the claims of the written word as though in fear of drowning in the musical sea.

brilliance: like "bursting ecstasy" and "sunrise," a normal Mallarmean definition of Wagnerian music—of the brasses in particular. See *Richard Wagner* (notes); and in *Ideas on Poetry:* "A gleam here or there, a sudden surge of music . . . seem to linger in a hesitating line like a forgotten sunset cloud"; or in *Mystery in Literature:* "Hesitations are folded darkly together . . . and then out of them arises an ultimate and essential brilliance."

retempered and purified: cf. in *Mystery in Literature:* "The written word . . . regains its rights as it stands beneath that fall of virginal sounds." The idea is important throughout Mallarmé's work. It means the purification and strengthening of word or of the poet himself. Cf.

the traitorous clown of *Le Pitre Châtié* (1864) "disappearing virginally" in the waves; the "purifying storm" of the present essay;
Hamlet and Ophelia, "jewel intact" and "never drowned"; and at the
end of *Music and Literature:* "The broil and tempest in which we
must stream."

Music must receive it: Freudian interpretations seem somewhat justifiable
here and in passages to follow: Music receiving poetry as water receives the diving poet, as "virginal sounds" fall on "the written word";
thus the "efficacies of life" will have "release." Cf. the "virgin space
. . . divided of itself" in *Mystery in Literature.*

no sonorous tumult: again, fear of the vague which is here synonymous
with dreams (i.e., with chance or the enemy of *the* Dream). Cf. Hamlet's famous soliloquy.

constant companion: for Mallarmé's view of the mob at the theater, see
Richard Wagner (notes). Everyone will share in the Ideal, but the
individual method of doing so remains superior. Let the mob listen
to the loud Wagnerian brass; the privileged reader will create his own
Ideal.

understanding attention: need it be recalled that the audience understood not a word of what he was saying?

seemingly impersonal: cf. in *Ideas on Poetry:* "I am . . . one of the ways
the Spiritual Universe has found to see Itself, unfold Itself through
what used to be me."

chef d'école: Mallarmé spoke rather more severely to this point in
Evolution when he said: "I detest 'schools' and everything resembling
schools."

must communicate their enthusiasms: as no one in the history of French
literature has done more generously than Mallarmé.

pitiful prince: Mallarmé's poet-as-Hamlet theme is of course implicit
here. Cf. in *Evolution:* "The poet . . . is a man who seeks out solitude
in order to sculpture his own tomb." See also Mallarmé's essay on
Hamlet.

something out of nothing: cf. the humor here to that in the first half of
Mystery in Literature.

M. Nordau: the pamphleteer Max Nordau (1849–1923), author of *Para-
doxes psychologiques,* habitually identified literature with his idea of
neurosis.

name nobody: Mallarmé is playing with the word *personne,* i.e., a
"nobody."

quite different brand: the first half of this satirical paragraph continues
the mockery which Mallarmé has been building up against Nordau,
but begins to be more labored, curt, obscure. The French becomes
correspondingly awkward.

some special moment: cf. Mallarmé's comment on this subject in *Hamlet:* "Well aware as he is . . . that the extraordinary moment is no longer, or not yet, at hand."

create a minority: see *Art for All, passim.*

twin fires: this refers to the stupidity of Nordau and of the newspaper writers.

somehow it will speak: yet another way of saying that dreams and chance can and must be eliminated. "The true function of literature," he exclaims in *Autobiography,* is the "Orphic *explanation* of the earth": i.e., music *and* words, vagueness *and* precision, the orchestral bird in flight *and yet* paradoxically digging its talons "deep within your earth."

neighbor to us all: Mallarmé continues in his *Notes:* "The eternal myth is communion through the Book, in Which each one of us has a total share." His sufferance (as well as distrust) of the mob is thus explained.

Because: cf. above, Mallarmé's beginning and end of a paragraph with the words "something else." It is not entirely clear why "because" receives similar treatment.

thoughts must ask: Mallarmé says in *Notes:* "If it is to be of value, a government must mirror the government of the universe. . . . The City [cf. *Richard Wagner,* notes] . . . is an abstract and superior place, located nowhere."

reborn as heroes: this rather curious paragraph recalls the power which Mallarmé attributes to Absence. He is not usually given to drawing images from the world of politics or city government, it may be added; but because, in the later portions of *Prosperous Trip,* he was concerned with questions of public domain, government subsidies, and the like, he is not averse to continuing that theme so long as it helps to explain the role of the Symbolist who, as he affirms, is actually Everyman.

Hamlet

Hamlet first appeared on November 1, 1886, in *la Revue Indépendante* as part of Mallarmé's *Notes on the Theater;* then in *Pages* (1891) and *Divagations* (1897).

The "prince of promise unfulfillable" is of course a partial self-portrait by Mallarmé the idealist, the hesitant, the lonely, the passionate, the remorseful, who stands—like Hamlet unable to "do it pat" upon the praying king—too often incapable of taking arms against the twenty-four letters of the alphabet, abolishing his imagined sterility, and writing the Poem.

Mallarmé's critical approach in *Hamlet* recalls *Ballets:* reporting on a performance, he moves lightly back and forth from the constructive to the humorously destructive; but the report remains a pretext for the exposition of his theory of the Drama.

See Charles Chassé, "Le Thème de Hamlet chez Mallarmé," *Revue des Sciences Humaines* (Jan.–March 1955), pp. 157–69.

autumnal Nature: this is in contrast to Her sterile winters (cf. *Le vierge, le vivace* of 1886) and the "serene irony" of Her "eternal blue sky" (*l'Azur,* 1864), autumn is the perfect season for the author of *Glory*—the moment preparatory to the "universal rite of the royal intruder." Like Mallarmé at Fontainebleau, Hamlet is going to intrude upon autumn's "purple, violet, pink, and eternally gold horizon."

ordinary cares and pleasures: i.e., the end of summer vacation, unwelcome beginning of the school year, and theater engagements. Note that Nature's display must take place in absence, without even the Poet's lucid eye.

dead-leaf bitterness: cf. in the early autumn poem *Soupir:* "The yellow agony of leaves wanders with the wind."

a few of my friends: i.e., poets or *quelques-uns.*

extraordinary moment: i.e., the realization of Mallarmé's perfect theater. Either the ideal has already been realized in a dark past, or else the hero's Monologue (see below) is "not yet at hand." Hence the banality of the Evenings.

child cut off: although the present essay is Mallarmé's only direct comment on the Hamlet theme, he had spoken indirectly in 1864 in the prose-poem *The Orphan Boy.* "Wandering about in black dress," the boy communicates the sense of loneliness and mourning in a setting of circus lamps and tents (see *The Punished Clown* below). Then, as Wallace Fowlie points out in his excellent analysis of the work (*Mallarmé,* Chicago, 1953, p. 243), "the first question dramatically opens up the Hamlet theme: 'Where are your parents' "?

having to appear: in *The Punished Clown* (a poem composed in 1864 and later revised), Mallarmé tells of the clown or poet-actor fearfully escaping from the ring, or stage, through the circus tent, diving

in water to find a new liberty and purification. "Bad Hamlet!" exclaims the remorseful poet, because he has fled from his duty to
"appear" (and from killing the king or writing poetry) and has found
only a new frustration, a new and multiple death: "It is as if, in
the wave, I were to construct innumerable sepulchres and disappear
within them in my purity." For further examples of the purification-
through-escape theme, see *Les Fenêtres* (1863), *l'Azur* (1864), *Soupir*
(1864), *Hérodiade* (1864–67), *Le vierge, le vivace* (1885), etc. For
further commentary on Mallarmé's portrayals of Hamlet, see Fowlie
(*op. cit.*) pp. 242–45; Albert Thibaudet, *La Poésie de Stéphane
Mallarmé* (Paris, 1926), pp. 382–83; Charles Mauron, *Introduction à
la Psychanalyse de Mallarmé* (Paris, 1950), pp. 157–62.

quickly disaccustomed: i.e., by a bad play.

screen of glory: i.e., the forest, as in *Glory*, which curtains the mystery
of autumn trees and sky.

indelicately palpable: cf. Mallarmé's humorous contempt for porter and
tourists (and his desire to be alone) in *Glory*.

yearly holocaust: i.e., autumn colors "burning" the leaves. Cf. in *Glory:*
"Torches burn all dreams."

moral space: the stage exists only in the vision of the spectator. Cf. in
Richard Wagner, Revery of a French Poet: "That fictitious stage of
vision which flashes in the glance of the audience."

fates allotted: the meaning of this sentence is beautifully illustrated by
Mallarmé's funeral oration for Verlaine. But his principal Hamlet-
heroes were Poe, Villiers de l'Isle-Adam, and himself.

the leading actor: Mounet-Sully (1841–1916).

symbolic relationship of characters: later, in *la Revue Blanche* of July,
1896, Mallarmé published the following short companion piece to
Hamlet, entitled *Hamlet and Fortinbras:* "An impresario from my
native province put on a performance of *Hamlet* and subtitled it:
'The Absent-minded Man.' His taste was typically French. I suppose he
hoped, in that way, to prepare the audience for Hamlet's uniqueness,
to show that Hamlet is the only one that counts! All who approach
him fade into the background, succumb, and disappear. The play is
the high point of the theater and, in Shakespeare's work, it lies halfway
between the old multiple-action method and the Monologue, the
drama of the Self, which belongs to the future. The hero is alone—
all others are secondary—and simply walks, reading in the book of
Himself, Who is a lofty and living Symbol. His glance ignores all
others. He is not content merely to show the solitude of a thinking
man. He kills indifferently; or, at least, people die around him. The
black presence of this doubter poisons the life out of every character

—he does not have to stab them all through the arras. To this
hesitater, of course, general Fortinbras lies in contrast. But that is
his only value. And when death (a phial, a pond of water-lilies, a foil)
is unleashed in rich display wherever that extraordinary human being
walks in sober dress, it is fitting (in the end and in the very last
analysis) that this sumptuous, stagnant, exemplary mass of murder
(which lies around Everyman who seeks solitude) should, so to speak,
flow vulgarly away in the wake of the army as it crosses and empties
the stage with its plain, dull destructive power, its drums and trumpets."

This passage provides perspective on Mallarmé's dramatic theory.
Just as in the ballet-arabesque there is a "strong-point," i.e., the
ballerina surrounded by her dance groups, so in drama the hero is
surrounded by lesser players. The result is a "symbolic relationship."
But whereas the ballet must live solely by its arabesque of groups
(for the ballerina cannot "write her poem" alone), the dramatic hero
should be ideally engaged in the "Monologue." Ideally, theatrical
performance will involve but one actor and a single, unending, silent
soliloquy. All other elements "fade into the background." *Hamlet*
approaches this ideal because of the several deaths caused by Hamlet
and his problem; because of the soliloquy form which isolates the hero
in such a way as to make him perfectly present to the spectator's
mind. Thus it appears—from *Ballets* and *Hamlet*—that the Mallarmean esthetic vacillated between the desired perfection of a constellation and that of a single star.

can divine them: a tactful device for passing from the review of the
performance to more important matters.

pernicious influence: in like manner, the matchless virtuosa Mademoi-
selle Mauri of *Ballets* made up for a "uniquely shreds and patches
performance" at the Eden Theater.

feather in his cap: cf. Mallarmé's *Un Coup de Dés* (1897): "solitary,
desperate feather" and "midnight cap" of the Hamlet-hero. In this
work—as well as in the earlier and equally difficult prose narrative
Igitur (1869?)—the Hamlet theme is present in the form of the poet-
hero preparing a last attempt to reach the Ideal through a Work—
or a throw of the dice—which will abolish the world of time and
chance.

image of himself: cf. the actor looking into "the time-honored text . . .
as in a mirror." Fowlie observes that "the tragedy of *Hamlet,* as
Mallarmé saw it, is a supreme expression of a man and his ghost
. . . of a man who acts out the torments of his spirit because he
is unable to live with them, of a man who creates a spectacle of

himself for others to see because he is no longer able to stand the reflection in his own mirror" (*op. cit.,* p. 244).

jewel intact: consciousness of the greatness of self, in the face of madness and grief, places Hamlet side by side with the jewel-like constellation of *Un Coup de Dés* which Mallarmé describes as "watching, doubting, wandering, glittering, and meditating."

Ballets

Ballets first appeared on December 1, 1886, in *la Revue Indépendante* as the second part of Mallarmé's *Notes on the Theater;* then in June–July, 1890, in *la Wallonie;* in *Pages* (1891); and in *Divagations* (1897).

Despite his unfamiliarity with the technical aspects of his subject (Proust, for example, was equally unskilled in musical technique), Mallarmé's *Ballets* and *Resources in the Ballet* still stand with the ballet studies of Paul Valéry and Jacques Rivière as the most perceptive and beautiful comments which the French have contributed to this form.

See *L'Ame et la Danse* in Valéry's *Eupalinos* (Paris, 1924) and Jacques Rivière in *Nouvelles Etudes* (Paris, 1947) under titles: *Petrouchka, Des Ballets Russes et de Fokine,* and *Le Sacre du Printemps.* For further discussion of Mallarmé's ideas on the ballet, see André Levinson, "Mallarmé métaphysicien du Ballet," *Revue Musicale,* November 1, 1923; Albert Thibaudet, *La Poésie de Stéphane Mallarmé* (Paris, Gallimard, 1926), pp. 364–83; Charles Mauron, *Introduction à la Psychanalyse de Mallarmé* (Neuchâtel, A la Baconnière, 1950), pp. 199–201; and Guy Delfel, *L'Esthétique de Stéphane Mallarmé* (Paris, Flammarion, 1951), pp. 181–83.

soft stretching: although he approaches ballet with strong intellectual intent to learn its lesson and relate it to literature, Mallarmé responds nonetheless to what Rivière would have called the "directions and animality" of the dance. The gestures of the nymphs in *The Afternoon of a Faun* are an excellent case in point. See Thomas Munro, "*The Afternoon of a Faun* and the Interrelation of the Arts," *Journal of Aesthetics* (December, 1951).

characters in costumes: Mallarmé is glad to be rid of these, but the ballet at the Eden has trappings of its own—the stars, for example.

dance of the constellations: the sentence is ironical; because, according to Mallarmé, the *corps de ballet* should assuredly "figure" this dance.

yellow muslin: let it glitter, he implies, but avoid the stagnancy.

certainly not drawn: i.e., as it should have been.

heroic refusal: a somewhat elaborate irony, equivalent to saying: "You couldn't fool *him* into thinking that two and two make four!"

fraction ad infinitum: each dance group, itself an arabesque, is linked to others by invisible and moving lines to form the great, "fractioned" arabesque, i.e., infinitely elaborated. Cf. in *Music and Literature:* "The omnipresent Line which runs infinitely from point to point in Its creation of idea."

not a girl dancing: cf. Valéry: "The soul is a woman dancing, yet who by a miracle ceases to be a woman." (*Op. cit.,* p. 17.)

writing with her body: cf. Valéry: "Their hands speak and their feet seem to write." (*Ibid.,* p. 19.)

came the Fable: for Mallarmé's views on this subject, see *Richard Wagner, Revery of a French Poet.*

The Two Pigeons: a fable of La Fontaine (Book IX, ii) which tells of a pigeon leaving home, being pursued by various dangers, and finally returning (half-dead and grateful) to his forgiving mate. Further on, Mallarmé makes fun of the fable's moral, i.e., "there's no place like home."

heavenly inability: this is an exquisite example of Mallarmé's attribution of positive power to absence or negativity. The French is: *"Cette espèce d'extatique impuissance à disparaître qui délicieusement attache aux planchers la danseuse."*

run on the flute: in other words, a "Bronx cheer" from the orchestra.

impatient wings: once again, note that some of Mallarmé's most beautiful sentences occur in his ballet criticism. The French: *"Elle invite, avec deux doigts, un pli frémissant de sa jupe et simule une impatience de plumes vers l'idée."* Cf. in *The White Water-Lily:* "Skirt flowing on the ground, floating about heel and toe as if to surround her step before she takes it, as . . . she walks forth with her cunning twin arrows."

perhaps the breeze: an ill-chosen example of incompatibility, so far as a dove is concerned.

remains to be found: Mallarmé is still struggling here toward a legitimate coalescence of various art forms.

few basic equations: cf. in *Music and Literature:* "The symphonic equation of the seasons." The metaphysician would reduce the spirit to a magic number. Cf. also in the *Coup de Dés:* "The unique Number which can be no other."

nameless, impersonal: in the same way, Wagnerian hero and music merge and become a depersonalized Figure or Symbol, according to Mallarmé.

the meaning of it: in his incisive *Positions et Propositions* (Paris, Gallimard, 1928), Paul Claudel observed: "Mallarmé was the first to face the outer world as if it were not a spectacle, but a text, and to ask: 'What does this mean?' " (p. 203).

Solemnity

Part one of *Solemnity* was composed in 1887 and first appeared in *la Revue Indépendante* in February of that year under the title *Notes on the Theater;* then in *Pages* (1891) and *Divagations* (1897). The remaining (and larger) portion appeared in the same review in June 1887 under the same title; then in *Pages* under the title *A Poetic Principle,* and in *Divagations.*

The two-part structure—pure irony followed by poetic theory—is especially reminiscent of *Art for All.* In both works, irony is at its most successful, its least offensively bitter. Since the second part is concerned with the "ministry of the poet," such unity as *Solemnity* may be said to possess lies in the arabesque of cardboard "gods" or "priests" of poetry, vestal virgins and druggists, temples or crypts of tenth-rate art. The work belongs generally with the great essays *The Book: A Spiritual Instrument, Crisis in Poetry,* and *Music and Literature,* in which the poet's fate is held again and again in awe, pity, and love. More particularly, it is Mallarmé's most protracted and sensitive treatment of the function and esthetics of rhyme.

pertaining to the Absolute: this is a delightful example not of Mallarmé's intellectual snobbishness (as the "mob" in his day naturally and seriously received it), but of the unique kind of mock snobbishness which will be found in all his humorous writing.

ineffectual trappings: all "trappings" are, by definition, "ineffectual," since the means and end of true poetry must remain immaterial.

Cf. *Ballets* and Mallarmé's humorous criticism of magic circles, stars in blue curtains, etc.

François Ponsard: (1814–67), a French playwright not considered among the best.

with the nonexistent: a good example of the occasional over-elaboration of Mallarmean irony. His thought is merely that "the present day" abounds in mediocrity which the past and future should be spared.

according to my Notes: not clear. Mallarmé is apparently referring—but to what purpose?—to his *Notes on the Theater,* the title under which *Solemnity* originally appeared.

. . . the God of poetry: Victor Hugo (1802–85), whom Mallarmé had always generally respected, although not so generally admired as Baudelaire or Poe.

Luce de Lancival (1764–1810), *"Campistron"* (1656–1723): inferior poets and playwrights.

She is in mourning: Mallarmé felt that true poetry was naturally cyclical and should therefore not be forced in an off-season or off-century. Cf. *Crisis in Poetry:* "French poetry is intermittent. It shines for a moment, dies out, and waits." The Campistrons are therefore guilty of bad timing as well as of bad verse.

Le Forgeron: a poem composed by Théodore de Banville (1823–91) who, with Villiers de l'Isle-Adam and Verlaine, became one of Mallarmé's close friends in Paris after 1871 (see E. Souffrin, "L'Amitié de Banville et de Mallarmé," *le Goëland* [July, 1943]). Mallarmé had admired him in his earliest years as the prince of Parnassians, and first mentioned him indirectly in 1862 in his review of the *Poésies parisiennes* of Emmanuel des Essarts. In 1864 he included Banville (with Théophile Gautier and Charles Baudelaire) in his *Literary Symphony,* a highly personal meditation on the beauties of those poets' work. Finally, in 1892, he renewed his praise in a short article on the occasion of the first anniversary of Banville's death. Despite these facts, it is quite evident that Mallarmé's admiration for him was little more than his usual and quite consciously undiscriminating admiration for the Poet as such. The friend or poetic figure were more deeply loved than the poetry itself, even in the case of Mallarmé's heroes, Baudelaire and Poe.

is not a poem: however "radiant" *Le Forgeron* may be, it is not going to keep its "critic" from indulging in general poetic theory. An essay's immediate subject—book, ballerina, musical composition—is never more than the briefest of pretexts for this man who was, after all, "incompetent in all matters not pertaining to the Absolute."

the dialectic of verse: Mallarmé is here separating, for purposes of demonstration, the substance or dialectic of poetry, i.e., its word-play, from poetic theory or concept. The two are, of course, inseparable, especially in his case, for whom poetry was by definition a disembodied reproduction of the Idea or universal Essence. Hence words are the stuff of poetry (as he once impishly informed Degas when the painter complained that he had "ideas" and still could not write poetry), but they are also what might be called Idea or Concept fragments.

yielding dreamer: Cf. *Crisis in Poetry:* "The poet gives over the initiative to words."

numerator of our apotheosis: Cf. in his *Ballets:* "Here, with their numbers, are the few basic equations of all fantasy."

two constituent elements: Cf. *Mystery in Literature:* "A virgin space . . . divided of itself, in solitude, into halves of whiteness."

their consonant equality: in a footnote, Mallarmé adds: "There lies the supremacy of modern verses over the ancient, which were unrhyming entities, filled once and for all with the metal which was their substance. The former, on the other hand, receive that metal or reject it, grow constantly, and proceed in musical fashion as does a stanza or a Couplet." The word "Couplet" is capitalized to reaffirm the supremacy of rhyme. Ancient verse "filled once and for all" should be contrasted with the image of the "supreme and nameless mold" of modern verse "which bears no palpable existence within itself."

its very substance: Mallarmé returns rather abruptly in this paragraph to the *Forgeron* and excuses himself for writing about anything so banal and materialistic as a plot.

discuss him here at length: this is another reminder (good-humored here) that the truly French mind cannot accept Wagnerian art as the Ideal, regardless of its influence on poetry. Cf. *Richard Wagner:* "It is not in this way that the strictly imaginative, abstract, and therefore poetic French mind shines forth. For that mind shrinks from Legend; therein it resembles perfect Art, which is invention."

which is the Book: Mallarmé's delicate way of saying that Banville is not a first-rate poet or Book creator.

ministry of the Poet: Mallarmé's capitals are to emphasize the fact that a Jubilee is a religious institution as well as a joyous celebration.

Richard Wagner, Revery of a French Poet

Richard Wagner first appeared in *la Revue Wagnérienne,* August 8, 1885; then in *Pages* (1891); selections in *Vers et Prose* (1893), and in *Divagations* (1897).

Mallarmé first became acquainted with Wagner in 1861 through Baudelaire's famous essay *Richard Wagner and Tannhaüser in Paris.* The following year, he added his name to those of Mozart and Beethoven in *Art for All.* But it was not until 1885 that French enthusiasm for Wagner reached its height and achieved literary expression in *la Revue Wagnérienne,* founded in that year. Several contributors to the review were friends or correspondents of Mallarmé, and it was undoubtedly through them that he gained whatever second-hand knowledge he needed to compose his revery. Only in the years following 1885 did he attend performances of Wagnerian opera and thus familiarize himself with the "Master's" actual accomplishment.

In January of 1885 Edouard Dujardin, editor of the review, had asked him to contribute an article. "I have spent all of yesterday and today on the study," replied Mallarmé on July 5. "It is half article, half prose-poem, but I haven't been able to finish it. It has been more difficult than anything I have ever done, I think. . . . I have never seen any Wagner, and yet I want to write something original, something accurate, something important on him. You must give me time." Two weeks later, the composition was sent off for publication.

For further comments on Mallarmé and Wagner, see E. Carcassone, "Wagner et Mallarmé," in *Revue de Littérature Comparée* (April–June, 1936), pp. 347–66; A. Thibaudet, *La Poésie de Stéphane Mallarmé* (Paris, Gallimard, 1926), pp. 364–83; J. Benda, *Domaine Français* (Geneva, 1943); and Hasye Cooperman, *The Aesthetic of Stéphane Mallarmé* (New York, The Koffern Press, 1933).

> *lonely Celebrations:* Mallarmé customarily makes liberal use of capital letters throughout this work. First, because many of his key words recur (Idea, Myth, Poetry, Monster, etc.); second, in order to set up a series of rallying points for the revery as a whole, a kind of constellation which will spiritualize it.

ceremonies of a day: see Mallarmé's three closing paragraphs of *Solemnity.*

unsuspecting womb: cf. in the late essay *Sacred Pleasure* (1893): "The mob . . . performs its function as guardian of mystery." Cf., also, the mob as prostitute, in *Mystery in Literature.*

neither this poet: cf. in *Hamlet:* "The extraordinary moment is no longer, or not yet, at hand."

clear and peaceful vision: this introduction to *Richard Wagner* is typically Mallarmean (cf. introduction to *Hamlet*): the poet sits quietly, almost anonymously, in his study, pondering the future and meaning of poetry. Notice the third person singular.

Chimaera: the Ideal is a paradise; but when the poet sees how unattainable it is, it becomes a cruel monster. Ultimately the poet will be devoured, but he can at least wound it before his death by coming face to face with it and writing poetry (or on poetry, as here). Cf. in *Music and Literature:* "Yet whatever the agony may be in which the Monster writhes (as, through Her golden wounds She pours the proof that She is always entire, always Herself). . . ."

varying reactions: in his later essay *Parenthesis* (1887) Mallarmé relates the disastrous reception that Wagner received from the demonstrative French "mob."

uneasy feeling: i.e., Mallarmé's feeling, as he reveals further on, despite his general admiration for any artist of lofty Ideal.

radiate: cf. Mallarmé's use of this word in his *Hommage* sonnet to Wagner in 1885: "The god Richard Wagner radiating a rite."

entirely new sense: i.e., in the best sense, like the Myth, hero, or Fable later on in the essay.

he will go along: cf. Mallarmé's tone in this paragraph to the scorn in *Art for All.*

empty, abstract, impersonal: cf. *Hamlet* and the "nameless, impersonal, glittering glance of absoluteness" of Mlle. Mauri in *Ballets.*

his lucid will: i.e., how could Wagner possibly re-create a Mallarmean Ideal and, at the same time, remain himself, i.e., "a tumultuous abyss of musical execution"? As a matter of fact, he could not; hence we find that Mallarmé has some misgivings in the latter part of the essay.

Oh, who can tell: cf. this parenthetical exclamation of Mallarmé's on Music's deep meaning with a similar passage in *Art for All:* "(And this has sometimes made me think . . .)."

deity draped: cf. in *Sacred Pleasure:* "The imperious velvet of a given pose will cut the shadow with a fold which has been colored by a given instrument."

on the pages of the Skies: like a constellation.

Poem or Ode: see *Solemnity.*

not any particular stage: Mallarmé is hinting here at an idea which he develops more fully and explicitly in the essay *Stage and Book:* namely, that the ideal book should contain within itself hero, place, stage, etc. Thus his basic objection to Wagner stems not from his disapproval of Legend *per se,* but from the too palpable realization which Wagnerian legend involves.

fictitious stage of vision: cf. in Mallarmé's essay *Limited Action* (1895): "A Place—as scene—appears; enlargement, for all of us, of the drama of the Self."

the City: a very vague and evanescent locale, in Mallarmé's imaginative scheme.

the City's people: cf. in *Music and Literature:* "Like a dutiful son or taxpayer, he willingly contributes what he owes to the common treasure."

be my witness: Mallarmé now returns to the first person, in preparation for the eloquence of the final paragraph.

Oh Genius: here in this magnificent closing paragraph, Mallarmé achieves the pure beauty or eloquence which place such "middle period" works as *Toast Funèbre* (1873) and *The White Water-Lily* among the finest writings in the history of the French language. The later (or post-1890) Mallarmé denies himself these qualities in his fanatic search for even greater perfection—with the exception of the *Verlaine* and one or two other brief instances.

trumpets abroad: the dome is round and golden, therefore sun-shaped and trumpet-colored. Cf. in *Hommage:* "trumpets loud and golden."

your welcoming fountain: cf. the closing sentence of *Parenthesis:* "To drink at the [Wagnerian] spring which our thirst has sought."

Verlaine

Verlaine first appeared in *la Revue Encyclopédique,* January 25, 1896; then in *la Plume,* February 1, 1896, and in *Divagations* (1897).

On January 10, 1896, Mallarmé and a small group of lesser writers stood in the Batignolles cemetery in Paris. Each in turn spoke a few words over the grave of Paul Verlaine. So ended, in fitting quietness and loyalty, a friendship begun thirty years before when Verlaine wrote Mallarmé at

Besançon. At first, there had been mutual admiration from afar; then, during the last years of their acquaintance, came mutual praise, understanding, and aid. Verlaine had included Mallarmé in his *Accursed Poets* (see *Autobiography*). Mallarmé, on the other hand, was concerned with his friend's physical and financial welfare and showed devotion which recalls his vigil at the bedside of the dying Villiers de l'Isle-Adam. This funeral oration is one of the most concise, moving, and yet serene of Mallarmé's prose works. It was followed, in 1897, by a well-known sonnet celebrating the anniversary of Verlaine's death.

For the definitive account of the Verlaine-Mallarmé relationship, see H. Mondor, *L'Amitié de Verlaine et Mallarmé* (Paris, 1939) and his "Verlaine et Mallarmé," *Revue de Paris* (February 1, 1940). See also André Gide, "Verlaine et Mallarmé," *La Vie des Lettres* (1914), pp. 1–23.

waters sweet: Mallarmé's praise does not fail to give sound judgment of the nature of Verlaine's poetry. Compared to his own highly structural and abstract verse, Verlaine's seems more melodic. The purely French quality has often recalled the personality as well as the ballads of François Villon.

profitable compromise: Mallarmé himself, of course, is probably the finest example in French literature of the uncompromising and absolute poet.

in all its horror: the first half of *Ideas on Poetry* best illustrates this situation.

insults must be borne: this mixture of courage and scorn reminds us of Mallarmé's lifelong faithfulness to the principles he set up in *Art for All.*

Ideas on Poetry

Ideas on Poetry includes letters (or parts thereof) selected from M. Henri Mondor's collection of Mallarmean correspondence under the title: *Propos sur la Poésie* (Monaco, Ed. du Rocher, 1953). This volume is itself a selection and, as the title suggests, contains those items which M. Mondor judged most likely to interest the general reader and lover of poetry. (Still other letters appear throughout M. Mondor's *Vie de Mallarmé* [Paris, Gallimard,

1941]; and Mallarmé's correspondence with Emile Zola, Henri Roujon, Georges Rodenbach, and others has appeared in various volumes within the past few years). I, in turn, have made selection from *Propos sur la Poésie,* omitting those portions which seemed to deal too particularly with Mallarmé's private life and relations. The positive bases for selection were the beauty and power of the letters. I also wished to present at least one or two examples from each of several Mallarmean periods, epistolary styles or critical topics; to observe, as M. Mondor suggests, the professor, the Symbolist, the Parnassian, the Tuesday evening speaker, or the critic.

Beginning with the voluminous correspondence of Madame de Sévigné in the seventeenth century, precious, tragic, or gossiping pens sought immortality day by day, and thus letter writing became an art in France. Several of Sévigné's contemporaries—Molière, Racine, etc.—made amusing although doubtful contributions to the genre with their hypocritical and fawning *placets* or dedicatory blurbs to protectors. Voltaire's gift for the concise and stinging phrase (highly appreciated by Mallarmé) fitted him admirably for this art. Here, too, the equally versatile and profounder Diderot naturally indulged his taste for dialogue and constructive criticism. The passionate Flaubert—more entirely himself in some of the greatest letters France has produced than in the tragically careful composition of his novels—showered on Louise Colet or George Sand the writer's agonies and ambitions and (like Mallarmé) uttered brief and powerful statements on art. More recently, the evasive Gide, the serious Claudel and Suarès, and the unctuous Proust (to mention only a few of the outstanding correspondents of our century) have occasionally resorted to this form to explain their lives, religions, and sicknesses.

The literary quality of these correspondences ranges from the carefully "composed" letter (or syntactical exercise) of Sévigné or Gide (well aware that their intimate thoughts and style would be read and discussed) to the marshalled arguments of Claudel, the impassioned pleas of Rivière, or the fussy and generally boring machinations of Proust, who fortunately saved his deep energies for his novel.

Mallarmé's correspondence has something in common with most (and with the best) of these traditions, but its great variety will not suffer any permanent or total assignment to a single category. For that reason, among others, it seems to me to be the culmination of this art in France. In his Introduction to *Propos sur la Poésie,* M. Mondor speaks predominantly of the elegance and gracefulness of these letters—qualities which are certainly characteristic of the later correspondence. In the eighteen-sixties, however, Mallarmé finds something akin to the passion of a Flaubert (all the while avoiding Flaubert's expansiveness), and with remarkable consciousness he distills that passion in the very midst of near madness or despair. Then, even in *that* midst, we will catch the measured note of irony and recall his admiration for Voltaire. Occasionally the French reader will meet Gidian turns of phrase, and then remember that Gidian syntax did not flee unscathed from the battles of Symbolism or from the quiet arabesques of the Tuesday evenings. The prevalent Mallarmean tact may possibly recall the indirections of the insidious Proust. But, impractical to the end, Mallarmé never attempted any flattery which could in any way be said to have served his ends. Nor, finally (and obviously), was it in his nature to Claudelize and convert.

The letters are almost always of the highest literary value; not that Mallarmé looked forward to their publication or advised his correspondents to keep them as treasures of his stylistic attempts (actually, some of his close friends were careless enough to lose or destroy large numbers of items from the moving correspondence of the 1862–70 period), but rather that, like Gide, he remained at his particular top of literary sovereignty in all genres. Despite his modest disclaimers, he felt obliged to encourage and advise the many young ardent poets who sought him out as the god of poetry. This being so, he framed his replies in a telling language of beauty and dignity which would serve as living symbols of his own poetic ideal. The result was, indeed, that on the weakest of pretexts the humblest of writers could elicit (depending on the Master's mood or age) some of the most elegant, delicately humorous, or moving passages of French prose.

Of the two main periods of this correspondence (1862–69 and 1870–98), the first is generally the more important and more characteristic of Mallarmé's originality as a correspondent. In those years, the man and poet were being born and developed. The birth pangs are recorded with a fulness surprising in a man usually so reticent, but also with a calm intensity and dignity which distinguish him absolutely from all other French letter writers or diarists. Somewhere in the vicinity of 1869, Mallarmé threw off the nervous depressions of the middle sixties. By this time, his originality was fulfilled. He left the provinces for Paris, firm in his poetic convictions and syntactically formed. His dark night had come and gone; his letters correspondingly lost the passion of the early days and acquired in exchange the gracefulness which links him to traditional French forms of letter writing.

> *Henri Cazalis:* (1840–1909), intellectual, lawyer, doctor, and poet, and one of the earliest and closest friends of Mallarmé, is perhaps better known by the pen name of Jean Lahor. He was the author of *Les Chants populaires d'Italie* (1865), *Melancholia, Henri Regnault, sa vie et son oeuvre* (1872), *Le Livre du néant* (1872), *L'Illusion* (1875).
>
> *Emmanuel:* Emmanuel des Essarts (1839–1909) had been appointed to

a teaching position at the Lycée de Sens in 1861, where Mallarmé was studying for the bachelor's degree. Their common love of poetry brought them together almost immediately, but des Essarts' "practical sense" (see letter to Cazalis, June 3, 1863) and superficial brilliance contrasted too violently with the other's timidity and disinterestedness ever to allow for a deepening of the friendship. In 1862, Mallarmé first appeared in print with two book reviews of des Essarts' *Poésies parisiennes*. Subsequently, the young men drifted apart, although they continued to correspond until 1874. Unfortunately, the only extant letters are des Essarts' to Mallarmé.

Springtime Spleen: Mallarmé called it *Spleen printanier, Vere Novo,* and finally *Renouveau*. Composed in May, 1862, it is a typical expression of the complex sterility which pursued the poet in the spectral forms of inability to put pen to paper, refusal to create imperfection, states of melancholia, ill health (headaches, nerves), and a Pascalian sense of the abyss.

Ideal: capital letters, as usual, expressive of the young poet's enthusiasm and of *the* Dream, *the* Ideal, etc.

Gautier: Théophile Gautier (1811–72), had been celebrated (along with Charles Baudelaire and Théodore de Banville) in Mallarmé's *Literary Symphony* of 1864. Mallarmé read his verse "at the feet of eternal Venus," admiring his sensitivity to color, rhythm, and synesthesia, as well as his "mysterious knowledge of the Word"—all these qualities combining to form the Parnassian poet in the best and fullest sense of the term. In his famous *Toast Funèbre* of 1873, Mallarmé chose Gautier as the incarnation of the artist possessed of the "mysterious power to see" and interpret the world around him; as the defender of art for art's sake; as the artist-atheist (see below); or, as he says elsewhere of himself, as "the mad, delightful hermit."

great art consists: in a penetrating analysis of Symbolism's procedures, Jacques Rivière observes: "The [Symbolist] first invents a story, but he doesn't have the time to tell it. . . . He doesn't see any reason for telling it. . . . It's behind him. And since he himself has gotten this far, why shouldn't the reader, too? . . . His true métier begins when he has gone beyond what he had to say; when all he has in front of him is the fleeing radiations emitted by the work he has suppressed." (*Le Roman d'Aventure* [Paris, Gallimard, 1947], pp. 237–38).

always omit the beginning: many disturbed readers of the late Mallarmé would protest that he omitted the middle of his poems as well. "Destruction was my Beatrice," he writes Lefébure, May 17, 1867. The history of Mallarmean poetry is in part the history of thought reduced to an inaccessible concentrate of ecstasy and darkness.

Hérodiade: usually paired or contrasted with *The Afternoon of a Faun,* both being long poems composed early in the author's career and considerably re-worked. In broadest terms, the former represents the sterile, wintry aspects of Mallarmé's character, the latter his softer, summery, happier, more sensual disposition. Their historical importance, as Mallarmé foresees here, lies in the originality of their language. For *The Afternoon of a Faun* and its contribution to French poetics, see *Evolution.*

excesses of my youth: the oft expressed sense of sterility which understandably fills the mind on the brink of artistic discovery leads the twenty-two-year-old Mallarmé to exaggerate past sins.

an amateur: cf. a later Mallarmé expressing his regret at having "accomplished nothing," when he had already composed some of the greatest poetry in French literature (letter to Paul Verlaine, April 7, 1884).

white paper: one of the strong points in the arabesque of virginity, sterility, death, mineral, ice, lake, swan, wing, etc.

solitude which quickens: this is a warning to Philistines that great artists, condemned to greatness by their instincts, inhabit ivory towers as prisons, not as homes.

strings stretch: cf. this paragraph to Mallarmé's essay *The Demon of Analogy.*

Eugène Lefébure: (1838–1908), still another early friend, with whom Mallarmé corresponded from 1862 to 1872. Lefébure eventually abandoned poetry and became an authority on Egyptian antiquity. See H. Mondor, *Eugène Lefébure, sa vie, ses lettres à Mallarmé* (Paris, Gallimard, 1951), and Mondor's "Stéphane Mallarmé et Eugène Lefébure," *la Table Ronde* (February, 1951), pp. 68–72.

Taine: Hippolyte Taine (1828–93), well-known critic and historian, author of works on English, French, and classical literature. Imbued with the positivist spirit, he believed that artistic nature and greatness could be ultimately and infallibly traced through an almost scientific study of the artist's race, surroundings, and time. So uncompromising a doctrine was bound to irritate the intellectually flexible and developing Mallarmé.

some strange way: cf. in Edgar Allan Poe's *Ligeia:* "There is no exquisite beauty without some *strangeness* in the proportion."

including E . . . : i.e., Emmanuel des Essarts. Mallarmé's irritation here represents a truer estimate of his friend's poetry than the empty and flowery praise of 1862 (see above).

a funeral pyre: cf. the tone of this passage to the opening pages of *Solemnity.*

the flute: a traditional definition of the poet: the man (or the faun) with the flute.

as pure theater: Théodore de Banville (see *Solemnity,* notes), flattered by Mallarmé's comments in the *Literary Symphony* and impressed by his poems and prose-poems, had hoped to have *The Afternoon of a Faun* performed at the Théâtre Français and urged Mallarmé to compose it as a dramatic monologue with sufficient plot to hold the spectator's attention. It turned out not to be "playable on the stage," since Mallarmé's natural subtlety of thought and syntax would have made the communication of any plot impossible. He abandoned it temporarily, re-worked it in 1866, hid it away, and finally had it published in 1876 (see *Evolution*).

spitballs: according to all reports of his contemporaries—and certainly by his own admission—Mallarmé was a very poor teacher; or rather, made no attempt in the classroom to be the inspired talker he became on Tuesday evenings. See Mallarmé's *Autobiography* (notes) and Léon-Paul Fargue, "La Classe de Mallarmé," *NRF* (May 1, 1941), pp. 641–49.

sanctuary: for Mallarmé's recurrent imagery of jewel, sanctuary, and temple, see *Solemnity* and *Art for All.* Cf. in *Hamlet* the "jewel intact in the midst of chaos."

Théodore Aubanel: (1829–86), was first introduced to Mallarmé in 1864. A native of Avignon, he was a member of the *Félibrige,* a society of poets formed in 1854 to preserve the Provençal dialect in French literature.

all its nakedness: the matter-of-fact tone of this and other sentences in the correspondence is the best guarantee that Mallarmé did see his poem in a literal sense understandable to mystics. Living in such constant familiarity with his own heights, he felt no need to expatiate or embroider.

musical overture: considerably more obscure than Mallarmé's "dramatic scene," this overture is (among other things) a remarkable complex of most of the key Mallarmean words: swan, wing, dawn, autumn, diamond, star, gold, snow, etc. Syntactically, it prepares and resembles the mature stylist.

tones of my despair: Mallarmé here reveals his overriding poetic ambition: to elicit a kind of nothingness (evanescent song infinitely interwoven, impalpable arabesque) from Nothingness (the human being's sense of the world). This and the following passage from *Music and Literature* are his finest and most originally phrased expressions of that desire: "For just as we have the right to elicit emptiness from ourselves (hampered as we may be by reality too solidly, too preponderantly enthroned in us), so do we act that a sublime attraction may lovingly deliver us from that reality—and yet be filled with it and shed glittering lights upon it through empty space and in wilful, solitary celebrations." For the Hegelian qualities of this thought, see Gardner Davies, *Vers une Explication rationnelle du "Coup de Dés"* (Paris, Corti, 1953), pp. 32–52.

glaciers: this is a key word in Mallarmean vocabulary, varying the theme of impersonality, sterility, purity, and beauty. It occurs notably in *Le vierge, le vivace* (1885), *M'introduire* (1886), and *Cantique de Saint Jean* (18??).

I have worked: This, Mallarmé's most difficult year, physically and mentally, 1866 was also the most revolutionary in the artist's troubled life.

risen from the dead: cf. in *Crisis in Poetry:* "In a crypt of equal silence lay the divinity of this majestic . . . idea."

mystery will spread: cf. Mallarmé's use of pyrotechnics in *Music and Literature.*

making other people think: Mallarmé always maintained, with general seriousness and occasional humor, that the obscurity of his work would at least help to develop careful, active readers. Considering the exegetic attention he has received in recent years, he was quite right.

like a sacred spider: cf. in Keats' letter to Reynolds, February 19, 1818: "Almost any man may like the spider spin from his own inwards his own airy Citadel—the points of leaves and twigs on which the spider begins her work are few, and she fills the air with beautiful circuiting. Man should be content . . . with the fine Web of his Soul and weave a tapestry empyrean." (Cited by L.-J. Austin, "Mallarmé et le rêve du *Livre*," *Mercure de France* [January 1, 1953], pp. 88–89, notes).

in Beauty's bosom: this passage is Mallarmé's clearest definition of the arabesque he sought to make of every poem and book of poetry. See also *Ballets* (notes) and *Crisis in Poetry, passim.*

Villiers de l'Isle-Adam: (1840–89), first met Mallarmé in 1864. They were to be life-long friends. Villiers is remembered today for his short stories and novel fantasies (he was the only Symbolist prose writer of considerable merit), and perhaps even more for a personality which dazzled such superior minds as Mallarmé's. The circumstances of his death offer an excellent illustration of Mallarmé's devotion to his friends and fellow artists (see *Verlaine*, notes). For a detailed analysis of their relationship, see G. Jean-Aubry, *Une Amitié exemplaire: Villiers de l'Isle-Adam et Stéphane Mallarmé* (Paris, Mercure de France, 1941).

even the Past: cf. the end of this letter: "Eternity has glittered. . . ." Mallarmé means not so much remembering, as dwelling in his extra-temporal universe of esthetic meditation.

thought itself through: the French reads, *"Ma Pensée s'est pensée,"* a purely Mallarmean comment expressing admirably his tension and sense of desperation in 1866. This mental process can be explained in metaphysical or psychoanalytical terminology, but with hardly sufficient clarity and concreteness for those who have never lived it. In any case, it seems to represent the extreme limits of the human power to abstract, self-mirror, self-deny. For the fascinating, deep, but troubled waters of Mallarmean metaphysics and epistemology, see R. G. Cohn, *L'Oeuvre de Mallarmé* (Paris, Librairie des Lettres, 1951), and Mallarmé's unfinished *Notes* of 1869.

matchless Nothingness: see above: *"tones of my despair."*

idea of that Universe: the problem was to write a poem which would be the exact mirror of the universe, encompassing its simplicity and complexities. Hence the arabesque of infinite movement, possibility, and relationships. Cf. in the *Coup de Dés:* "The unique Number which can be no other," and *Ballets* (notes).

I had no Mind: i.e., the thinking out, the concretion of the experience (in the form of poems and metaphysical structures) necessarily came afterwards, as, for example, the Pascal *Pensées* followed the *Mémorial*, or the "explanations" of a Saint Theresa, a Saint John of the Cross, or a Simone Weil followed their privileged moments.

whatever sense of Time: as with other writings, this beautiful letter can be variously interpreted by doctors, metaphysicians, psychoanalysts, artists, or philistines. (See, for example, J. Fretet, *L'Aliénation poétique* [Paris, Janin, 1946]). And perhaps, too, by mystics, who would confirm Mallarmé's nearly physical sense of the *full weight* of emptiness, his immersion in the horror inspired by a vision of the universe. In his own fashion, Mallarmé lived the ecstasy of fear and fascination which Pascal distilled in the cry: "The eternal silence of these infinite spaces terrifies me."

François Coppée: (1842-1908), a minor "people's poet," and an acquaintance rather than a close friend of Mallarmé.

leave Tournon: parents' complaints about Mallarmé's teaching had compelled school officials to dismiss him.

self-mirroring: cf. the "walls of a cave" in *Mystery in Literature* (notes).
these last months: cf. the letter of September 24, 1866, to Villiers de l'Isle-Adam.

I fortunately defeated: this quite extraordinary and occasionally baffling passage (along with the *Toast Funèbre,* of 1873) has usually been cited as proof of Mallarmé's atheism. This opinion is without any doubt strongly based on his desire for independence (see letter to André Rossignol, May 24, 1893), his pride in the poet's life, his determination to solve through poetry what seemed to him to be the essential problems of the world. On the other hand, he was acutely aware of his relationship with a higher power; in fact, nothing was more *real* for Mallarmé than the emanations of that power in the form of Infinity and Nothingness. To defeat, to imitate, or to reproduce those emanations was his poetic ambition. Apart from that, we actually know little or nothing about his religious convictions; the question of the Christian (or any other) *ethic* is beside the point (save with respect to his personal conduct, which his contemporaries found exemplary). So, at least, I should interpret the *oublions* of *Catholicism.* The metaphysical problem is raised only with a view to an esthetic solution. There is no evidence that Mallarmé was concerned to defeat the Catholic God; his struggle toward a perfect comprehension of the universe and of nothingness does not involve a prior elimination of religious beliefs—beliefs which, beyond the esthetic sphere, he may well never have entertained. What he had to defeat primarily was the Power (of what nature or personality, he cared not) Who "once unleashed Infinity," as he remarks in *Music and Literature;* "Whose rhythm . . . can be rendered by the fitting words of our daily tongue"; the Power incarnate in Chance and dreams; in short, the Chimaera whom he fights in *Richard Wagner, Crisis in Poetry, Music and Literature, Catholicism,* or *passim.* In the present passage, that Chimaera is called "God," but remains a palpable, winged Monster, incarnation of the reality which Infinity represented to his mind. Likewise, in *Crisis in Poetry,* Mallarmé is resigned to nature's law (i.e., Chance, Infinity, etc.) which decrees that "we have no sufficient reason for equating ourselves with God." In one sense, then, he cannot defeat God (is he an atheist at that moment?) because "languages are multiple" (a kind of original sin in the poet's world), because each has its own perverseness, etc.; but with *verse* instead of words, and with a "unified view of the universe," he can practice his own religion to perfection by writing a poem (constellation, etc.) victorious over the Infinite, with which he was both concerned and unconcerned.

For another example of the bird-defeat combination, see *Le vierge, le vivace* (1885) in which a swan-poet is caught fast in the ice of its own sterility.

my Venetian mirror: Mallarmé's version of the Narcissism (see also *Hérodiade* and *Igitur*) which is to be found especially in the thinking of Baudelaire, Valéry, and Gide.

one of the ways: this partial identification of his now impersonal self (i.e., his no longer imperfectly human self) with the Universe further describes the nature of Mallarmé's defeated God. If the Universe will continue to "unfold Itself" through him, he will achieve universal understanding and beauty. "Defeating" God and the Universe really means absorbing or resorbing the poet into the defeated. The role of the (here) mystic Mallarmé is passive (or defeated), as is usual in mystical experience. When the vision has passed, he will turn to action through words.

nothingness to come: Mallarmé usually scorns to capitalize "nothingness" when it means merely physical death.

the Great Work: cf. in *Autobiography:* "I have always dreamed of, and attempted, something else; patient as an alchemist . . . in order to feed the furnace of the Great Work."

was my Beatrice: the extreme conciseness of a Mallarmé poem is, of course, closely connected with the desire to seize and reproduce Nothingness.

looked upon it: and, like the God of Genesis, "saw that it was good." See above: "*all nakedness.*"

in my chest: critics have smiled, perhaps rightly, at Mallarmé's constant fear of pulmonary disease. It is a case of the Symbolist stealing the Romantic's thunder. As it turned out, finally, he died of laryngeal trouble.

with coffee: unlike Poe and Baudelaire, Mallarmé was able to "get his brain going" with the most innocent of liquids.

produce a vibration: this is one of the very few ridiculous passages in Mallarmé. But perhaps the physiology of the envisioning mystic or cabalist must submit to such "shattering" procedures.

as a legacy: Baudelaire had already translated the majority of Poe's prose works into French. See Léon Lemonnier, "Baudelaire et Mallarmé traducteurs d'Edgar Poe," *les Langues Modernes* (Jan.–Feb., 1949), pp. 47–57.

sell my goods: Mallarmé never wrote this work, but he often examined the role of the mob in the presentation of a work of art. See the late essays *Sacred Pleasure* (1893), *Catholicism* (1895), and *Richard Wagner, Revery of a French Poet.*

drive the monster: here he means the mob. Cf. the Hydra-mob in the
Tomb of Edgar Poe (1876).

exquisite collection: this is the first in a series of flattering remarks to
his fellow poets. The poetry of Coppée deserved no such praise; but,
as a friend observed, Mallarmé was "the politest man of his generation."

Emile Zola: (1840–1902); for comments on Mallarmé's connection with
him, see *Evolution* (notes) and *Dix-Neuf Lettres de Stéphane Mallarmé
à Emile Zola* (Paris, La Centaine, 1929).

this work of yours: i.e., *L'Assommoir,* now considered to be one of Zola's
three or four great novels.

part I like best: Mallarmé's judgment is sound. Critics generally find
the first part of the book superior to the rest.

Léo d'Orfer: editor and associate editor of two literary reviews, *la Vogue*
and *le Scapin,* in 1886. Mallarmé's letter is a reply to d'Orfer's request
for a "Definition of Poetry."

René Ghil: (1862–1925), one of the first to attend the Tuesday evenings,
he became Symbolism's leading theorist in 1886 with the essay *Traité
du Verbe.* The work is now famous for Mallarmé's preface (see *Crisis
in Poetry,* notes). Like Mallarmé, Ghil was anxious to create a single
"Great Work," but his "verbal instrumentation" and "colored music"
came to naught.

recovering everything: see *Music and Literature* (notes), *Art for All,* and
Richard Wagner.

Gustave Kahn: see *Crisis in Poetry* (notes).

which other ears: cf. this letter on official and unofficial verse with *Crisis,
Evolution,* and *Music and Literature.*

Emile Verhaeren: see *Crisis* (notes).

the poet disappears: see *Crisis* (notes).

torrents of their own storm: cf. in *Solemnity:* "That metaphorical sky
which mushrooms out in the vicinity of the poem's lightning"; and
in *Crisis:* "Thus Mystery bursts forth ineffably throughout the heavens
of Its own impersonal magnificence."

Henri de Régnier: see *Evolution* (notes).

fluid quality: see Mallarmé's letter of January 22, 1888, to Emile Verhaeren.

Jean Moréas: see *Evolution* (notes).

a foreigner: Moréas was of Greek extraction. Mallarmé never hesitated
to point out—politely but firmly—that a foreigner's knowledge of
French could not be perfect. See the letter of January 27, 1876, to
Charles Swinburne, in M. Mondor's edition of Mallarmé's letters,
Propos sur la Poésie.

Paul Valéry: (1871–1945), ranking among the greatest critics and prose stylists in French literature, was also an outstanding poet, perhaps excessively influenced by Mallarmé. A late-comer to the Tuesday evenings (1890), he nevertheless became Mallarmé's closest literary associate and staunchest defender. His interest in the processes of poetic creation and his intellectual approach to life and art were bound to attract him to the *Maître.*

in every written work: cf. in *Autobiography:* "The Book . . . has been attempted by every writer, even by Geniuses."

plagiarize: i.e., the Poet must recover "everything that Music once took from us."

Vielé-Griffin: (1864–1937), Symbolist poet of American origin and faithful admirer at the Tuesday evenings.

scattered whispering: "En l'éparse chuchoterie de ma solitude," goes the French here, in typically *précieux* and Mallarmean fashion.

interminable study: it is known that Mallarmé devoted much of his time to special linguistic study in preparation for the "Great Work." Unfortunately, he asked his wife and daughter to destroy the major portion of his notes, since they remained, in his eyes, unfulfilled by such a work. We possess only a few scattered pages of these notes, some of them written during the 1865–69 period, others in the nineties, all of them dealing rather abstractly and obscurely with language, word, and science.

state of purity: cf. the statement in *Crisis in Poetry:* "The poet must establish a careful relationship between two images"; and: "The poet [must not] fill the delicate pages of his book with the actual and palpable wood of trees."

Charles Bonnier: this letter of 1893 is a part of the brief correspondence between Mallarmé and Bonnier, a Frenchman teaching and writing at Oxford at the time. Bonnier was responsible for arranging Mallarmé's trip to England the following year. See *Music and Literature* (notes).

to go together: cf. in *Crisis in Poetry:* "An idea is naturally fractionized into several motifs of equal value which must be assembled."

establishes the poem's: cf. in *Crisis:* "The perfect symmetry of verses within the poem, of poems within the volume, will extend even beyond the volume itself."

tend to neglect: tactful to the very end (especially with an old friend), Mallarmé terms "weariness" the endless struggle that he (as well as Baudelaire and Rimbaud before him) waged against the often purely "lulling" verse of the Romantic poets.

André Rossignol: an unidentified correspondent.

Charles Morice: see *Evolution* (notes).

Poe's view: principally expressed in his essay *The Poetic Principle,* which condemns "the heresy of the Didactic" and the attempt to reconcile the "obstinate oils and waters of Poetry and Truth."

André Gide: (1869–1950); the famous French novelist, critic, and man of letters came under the influence of Symbolism early in his career. He attended the Tuesday evenings in the early nineties.

the poem is now: i.e., the *Coup de Dés,* which first appeared in May, 1897, in *Cosmopolis.* For its pagination, blanks, etc., see *The Book: A Spiritual Instrument* (text and notes).

your Dawns: Mallarmé rather tactfully ignores the fact (which must have irritated him) that Verhaeren's drama was a tribute to social revolution and similarly unpoetic subjects.

spiritual theater: see *Richard Wagner* (notes).

Index